To Mary,
May this book inspire!

Charles Tyr

To Mary,
With best wishes for your journey
and the meaning you bring to life.

Cathy

THE CARMEN PORCO STORY:
JOURNEY
TOWARD JUSTICE

A biography by

CHARLES TAYLOR

ISBN: 978-1-54397-419-5 (print)
ISBN: 978-1-54397-420-1 (ebook)

DEDICATION

To all the souls who agree with Reverend Carmen Porco that we must work for a more just world that benefits all of us, based on our shared humanity.

ACKNOWLEDGMENTS

Many people contributed to the completion of this book. First and foremost is Carmen Porco, who patiently sat through hours and hours of interviews over a six-month period. I would also like to acknowledge the following individuals for their help in improving this manuscript: Camilla Rucinski, Phyllis Sides, Elizabeth Johanna, Kathy Martinson, Margaret Porco, and Judy Davidoff.

I must give a special shout-out to three extraordinary colleagues who helped me draft this book: Susanna Daniel, Jonathan Gramling, and John Porco. Susanna is the author of *Stiltsville*, winner of the 2011 PEN/Bingham Award, and *Sea Creatures*, a Target Book Club selection. She is also the cofounder of the Madison Writers' Studio, a high-level private writing workshop in Madison, Wisconsin, and has recently finished her third novel. Jonathan is the publisher and CEO of *The Capital City Hues* and an award-winning journalist, and his contribution, improved the manuscript. John Porco, teacher and scholar, is the son of Carmen and provided invaluable insight and organizing skills.

CONTENTS

FOREWORD

Over the past few years, I have had the pleasure of working with Dr. Charles "Chuck" Taylor. He produced several documentaries that allowed me to share the story of my low-income housing ministry, which empowers the residents by offering them an array of resources and not just shelter.

During one of our frequent lunches, as I was giving Chuck an update on my ministry, he asked me questions that caused me to reflect on periods of my life from long ago. He introduced the idea of telling my personal story, through a biography, to further my vision of sharing with the greater community a new way of ministering to the poor.

Initially, I felt overwhelmed and confused about the idea, as it was one thing to share my story with a trusted friend but quite another to make my story into a book and share it with the public. Was my life that unusual and unique? Would my story truly be of value to others? Obviously he convinced me to move forward.

I agreed to meet Chuck weekly for the next six months so that he could interview me. His probing questions allowed me to reveal a great deal about myself and my beliefs. Through telling my stories to him, I better understood why I often viewed myself as an outsider and so readily identified with the struggle of other oppressed groups. I realize that this can be a universal experience for many who view themselves as marginalized, but the words suddenly held deeper meaning when they were attached to "my story."

There are so many lessons I learned from doing this book and taking this look back at my life. I did not make it this far on my own. Further, upon reflection, I was able to identify extraordinary people, family, ministers, educators, and lay people who shaped my thinking and helped me develop a more inclusive approach to life. You'll meet many of them in this book, and I will always be indebted to them. I'm hopeful that my sense of humbleness and gratitude for their many contributions comes through in this book.

I discovered great insights into why I am the way I am and how I developed over the years. I learned that being raised in a negative environment is not an excuse for how one ends up in life. We can use our past as a crutch or as a stepping-stone to inspire others. My parents did not have an easy life themselves. Nonetheless, they demonstrated love and discipline in the best way they knew how. Love can and does conquer the devastating effects of violence, oppression, and exclusion.

My unshakable desire for seeking justice started in my hometown of Weirton, West Virginia. Growing up in a community of poverty caused me to think differently about life. The trauma of seeing how the *least of these* were treated with injustice and indignity caused a great depth of despair within my soul but also motivated me to proudly champion the dignity of the poor for the rest of my life. The people I grew up with were just as decent and perhaps more generous with what little they had than people who were much better off financially.

Growing up in a barroom brought out both my good and bad traits. Unfortunately, it took the death of my best friend, Bobo Young, before I began questioning my life choices and opening my heart to Christ. Bobo was just one of many African Americans who back then and still today remain a big part of my life. They helped me to understand our shared humanity and brought to life the notion that we're all God's children.

There was a period in my life where I tried to be a traditional pastor but quickly learned that the ministry that resonated with my soul lay outside of the structured church. In fact, the more I got involved with the traditional church, the more disappointed I became with organized religion. As I watched the mainstream church address issues of poverty and racism, it seemed the church was ignoring systemic issues of injustice or just paying lip service to these deep-seated challenges. I felt that pastors needed to reach out to people where they found them in pain. That's what the church should be about, and that was to be my calling and life's work.

Following that calling and life's work resulted in the blessings of a successful ministry of transforming low-income housing by building community learning centers and aggressively challenging the status quo of traditional housing management. I have tried to fight the good fight. But it is not enough to make a difference in individual lives; we must also focus on transforming our institutions so they began to dispense justice and opportunity. Until our institutions are effective at generating inclusion and trust, we will suffer the same dysfunctional outcomes. Prisons will grow, public schools will deteriorate, health systems will fail, and our democracy will be threatened.

It is my hope that as you read my story, my life lessons will assist you on your personal journey. It is also my wish that my story inspires you to make a difference and join me in my search for justice. That is the True Church that I aspire to.

— Carmen Porco

INTRODUCTION

My friend Akbar Ally introduced me to Reverend Carmen Porco a few years back. I was immediately struck by Carmen's passion and commitment to social justice and his refreshing view of what he calls the "True Church"- a church that isn't limited to a building but, rather, one that is found in the streets, the barrooms, and, in his case, low-income housing complexes. He believes that pastors should minister to people as they find them because everyone is worthy of grace.

Although he has a master of divinity degree from Andover-Newton Theological Seminary, Carmen is not your traditional pastor. For more than 40 years, his pulpit has been his housing ministry and his congregation his residents. Carmen says many churches have the right intentions, but they don't risk anything in the street, where people are hurting. They offer what he calls "cheap grace."

In Carmen's experience, cheap grace allows churches to pay lip service to serving the poor while not really making the financial, moral, or social commitment to addressing their needs. He argues this lack of commitment among the country's religious communities helps support systems that keep people oppressed, rather than move toward the type of systemic change that is needed to bring about justice and equality.

I was also drawn to Carmen's compassion for people and his life-long work in helping low-income families improve their lives through his housing ministry. Once I found out more about the significant work he was doing in this area, I knew it was important to share his ministry, but I also knew that it would take time for Carmen to allow me to tell his story. It took nearly two years to convince him to let me produce a series of films on the great work he was doing in his low-income housing properties in Madison and Milwaukee, Wisconsin.

Carmen didn't want the spotlight, but I told him something my grandmother used to tell me: "A light will shine anywhere, so let your light shine. It may inspire others to pick up the mantle and continue your work."

Carmen grew up in a barroom on the poor side of town in Weirton, West Virginia. As a young gang leader, he lost his best friend to gang violence, which propelled him to preach in a pulpit before he was 15 years old. His Italian parents ran a small bootlegging operation out of their home before opening a tavern years later. All types of people streamed in and out of their bungalow on Division A Street in Weirton to buy liquor. Many would sit around "Big Bertha," a pot-bellied stove with rails that customers warmed their feet on, and tell stories while drinking and playing cards.

As a child, Carmen made authentic friendships with African Americans and discovered that he shared a common bond with them. His early understanding that all people are connected is one of the values that have guided his life. Carmen believes that our neighborhoods will only become true communities when we discover our interdependence.

Carmen had a front row seat during the civil rights era and worked directly with Father James Groppi and others during the marches for open housing in Milwaukee, Wisconsin. He was also deeply influenced by creative thinkers and leaders in the integrated housing and antipoverty movement, people like James Rouse and Herbert Gans.

Carmen has worked for the American Baptists organization in their housing ministry department for most of his career, which spans more than 40 years. Initially trained in his 20s to manage their low-income housing properties across the country, Carmen discovered that public housing could be a vehicle for transformative change. He says housing is a core element of life and society. "It is an issue of acceptance, belonging and human rights. Housing is the thread of the quilt of community," he states.

Carmen believes that public housing complexes for low-income residents must do more for people in need than just offer shelter. "These properties that are benefiting from government subsidies should provide a comprehensive array of social and educational services onsite so that poor people have the resources necessary to improve their lives."

Carmen finally got a chance to test his beliefs in Madison, Wisconsin, where he created a unique housing management model. Not only did he build learning centers and hire residents to staff the centers, but he also developed a scholarship and internship program for young residents. For the first time, the low-income housing community had an institutional base with a high degree of resources dedicated to helping them succeed.

As a result, the high school graduation rates of his residents have skyrocketed; the dropout rate has dramatically declined; crime has gone down; and nearly one out of every four resident households has a family member in college. The residents who live in the properties have both hope and opportunity, and that alone should make his model worth replicating. Unfortunately, the U.S. Department of Housing and Urban Development has not shown to date a willingness to adopt Carmen's comprehensive housing management model at the national level.

When Carmen first arrived in Madison, activists and community leaders, including Mayor Paul Soglin, didn't know he held such progressive views and called him a "scum lord," since the properties he came to town to manage were notorious for treating poor people badly. Madison activists also didn't know that Carmen knew how to fight back. Using his considerable experience and political savvy, Carmen soon went from being called a scum lord to being known as a champion for the poor. Since then, the Madison community has bestowed upon him several significant awards, culminating recently with the Rev. Dr. Martin Luther King, Jr. Humanitarian Award that he cherishes above all others. Telling Carmen's story is important because he is an ally who lives his faith and demonstrates that hope can triumph over despair.

When I was contemplating writing Carmen's life's journey, I knew that it would require a considerable time commitment and that I would need help. Fortunately, I was able to find Susanna Daniel, a talented and gifted author, to help me tell Carmen's story. I interviewed Carmen for hours at a time over six months, and Susanna helped me draft each chapter. Carmen's son John Porco also contributed greatly to the final draft and helped tie it all together. Jonathan Gramling's fine writing skills undoubtedly improved the final draft as well. As a result, I am able to give you a portrait of Carmen Porco, the man, and his life's journey.

— Charles Taylor, author

CHAPTER ONE

Italian Roots

SOME PEOPLE ARE BORN INTO A LIFE OF PRIVILEGE IN A safe community with good schools and hope for the future. Others are born into the crucible—a hot mess of historical circumstance, poverty, suspicious cops, and miseducation—while facing a strong headwind of injustice and discrimination. Although Carmen Porco was born into America's dark crucible, his family's roots began earlier—in the old country.

His father, Carmine Porco, was born in Belmonte Calabro, Italy, in 1905. The Porcos farmed, far from Rome or any other large metropolitan area. The political chaos of World War I and the threat of anarchist bomb attacks brought the fascist movement right to the doorsteps of rural Italy as well.

In 1922, Carmine was away from home studying to become a priest when the fascists marched in Rome to take control of the country. They also raided the countryside, with fascists loyal to Mussolini taking over city councils and other local governments throughout Italy—killing many of the local leaders who opposed them. This change in government found the Porcos on the losing side of politics. Everything fell apart the weekend that Carmine went home to make sure his family was safe. Like so many other Italians, Carmine, along with his father and brothers, was forced to flee.

Although Carmine and his brothers successfully escaped, they didn't escape tragedy along the way, and the event shaped Carmine's view, and mistrust of, government power and authority for the rest of his life. Years later, Carmine was always quick to remind people that the government was not to be trusted, no matter how democratic it looked. As the Porco boys ran from their homestead in Belmonte Calabro toward the port city of Naples, they watched their father die from wounds he had suffered during one of the fascist raids.

The brothers' last act together as a family was to bury him in a ditch. Then, they ran separate ways. Three of the brothers went to South America, while Carmine and his two brothers Frank and Joe stowed away on the S.S. *Providence* bound for New York, often hiding in containers and cargo holds or anywhere else they wouldn't be found.

They arrived at Ellis Island on a cold November day in 1922. Carmine Porco was only 17 years old. This was the first time he had been someplace where the temperature got below freezing. Like the millions of immigrants before him, he sought a better life in America. Unlike the white generations before him, who were given free land or jobs in agriculture, Carmine's cohort of immigrants discovered that America no longer needed farmers to break sod and cultivate her wildlands. He was not welcomed with open arms, but with suspicious glances and warnings to keep to his own. For many Italians, the mafia was the only way to integrate into the fabric of American life. At least initially, this was no different for Carmine.

Carmen recalls stories of his father's arrival in America. "They were picked up by a 'mafia family' in New York when they debarked from the ship; Dad got intertwined in that for a while. He got into a 'family' where he had to be tough and mean. He proved to be damn good at it." Mafia families in America took on the role of the extended family for many Italian Americans arriving in the new country, but for Carmine, his search for a better life in America didn't end in New York, but further westward. He and his brothers already had a relative living in the Ohio River Valley area of Pennsylvania, where there was a growing Italian-American community.

"The mafia really wasn't what he wanted to be involved in for any extended period of time. And then somehow he not only had the strength to break away from it, but also the credibility to be able to do that and not get killed," Carmen says. "He figured that with his hard-work ethic, there had to be a better life." Carmine was able to escape from the mafia life, though not without the experience leaving permanent emotional scars.

Less than a year after he had arrived in New York, Carmine and his brothers headed to a large Italian community in Fairmont, West Virginia, and they found work in the coal mines. Carmine Porco had become a hard man, his character forged by the violence in Italy as well as his introduction to the mafia in New York. He had come to the United States at a time when African Americans and immigrants from countries like Ireland and Italy were used to fuel America's industrial revolution, working the filthy, life-shortening jobs in the coal mines and steel mills of West Virginia and Pennsylvania.

In Fairmont, Carmine met Theresa Rotell, a fiery first-generation Italian girl. Her family had emigrated from Italy, with the bulk of Italian immigrants, a generation prior to Carmine. Theresa, who would later be called Daisy, or Miss Daisy, by everyone who knew her, helped her mother, Genevieve, run a boarding house for coal miners, washing and ironing clothes for the boarders. She had the same tenacious work ethic as Carmine.

Unlike Carmine, whose outlook had been shaped by violence, Daisy was born into a family that had managed to scrape out a living by working together. Carmine worked to survive, whereas Daisy worked to care for others—first at her parent's boarding house, then later in her own home as a landlord, daughter, mother, and care provider. She took care of everyone from her kids, to her mother as she grew old, to her sister, and to her sister's kids.

After a short courtship with Carmine, Theresa became pregnant, and Genevieve told Carmine to marry her—and he did. At the age of 16, Daisy was married to Carmine and continued helping to run the boarding house while also taking care of her firstborn child—Joseph, nicknamed Jojo—who had been born with Down syndrome.

Within two years of being married and having his first child, Carmine moved his family to Weirton, West Virginia, a town of about 24,000 residents, where the Weirton Steel Mill had recently expanded operations. Mill work had a reputation for being less grueling and better paying than coal mining. The family settled into a two-story bungalow in the hardscrabble north side of town, on Division Street. It was here in 1928 that they welcomed their second child, a boy they named John, whom everyone called Pat.

The town of Weirton developed on the eve of World War I when the steel mill opened. At its height, the mill employed as many as 12,000 workers. When the town incorporated, the city council was made up mostly of mill executives. As Carmen puts it, "What Weirton Steel Mill wanted, Weirton Steel Mill got."

Weirton was divided into four distinct neighborhoods. There was Maryland Heights, where the wealthiest citizens lived; Calico Hill, an African-American area; Weirton Heights, an upper-middle-class neighborhood; and the North Side, which was home to poor people of every race—including Carmine and his family. The North Side neighborhood was all residential, except for some businesses on the main street. Despite being poor, everyone in the North Side neighborhood owned their own house, which they often built by themselves over time with whatever materials they could get ahold of. The kids played in the streets, and walked to school with the shrieking whistles that signaled shift changes at the mill.

As for Carmine, coal mining had given him a new start in America, but it wasn't destined to be his future. He had brought one skill with him from his childhood in Calabria, and this skill would put food on his family's table for the rest of his life: making wine. Carmine had started making wine in their house in Fairmont while he was working in the coal mines. After the move to Weirton, he continued to make wine in his basement during his time off from the steel mill. Soon he and Daisy were selling jugs of red wine, which he called "Dago Red." Carmen recalls his father complaining about Americans who asked for white wine: "What's the matter in this country? This country is soft. White wine is for the weak." In addition to the homemade wine, the Porcos sold fifths of liquor and six-packs of beer. West Virginia was a "dry" state back then, so anyone wanting to drink alcohol was forced to either cross state lines to obtain it or buy it from bootleggers. The Porcos' business was a small-time bootlegging operation at first, but with Daisy's help and a steady stream of mill workers coming off all three shifts, the business grew fast. So did their family.

Babe

Daisy gave birth to four boys in a span of 22 years. Birthing children is always a challenge, but Carmen's birth was by far the most harrowing for the Porco family. "*Porca miseria!*" Daisy cursed in her native Italian as doctors packed her in ice to slow down the labor and ease her pain. "*Dio aiutami!*" God help me! After three days of hard labor, Carmen was born.

"Momma always told me she felt like I was trying to kill her," Carmen says. "She took great joy in reminding me how hard she'd worked to make sure I got here." It was Daisy who gave Carmen the nickname that his family and friends would call him throughout his childhood. Since he was the youngest of her babies, she called him Babe.

Carmen "Babe" Porco was born on April 29, 1947, in a hospital in Steubenville, Ohio, two miles from his hometown of Weirton, West Virginia. Daisy and Babe's father, Carmine, brought him home to a dilapidated two-story A-frame bungalow on Division Street. The neighborhood was inundated by yellowish-brown soot and the persistent rumble of the nearby steel mill. His family were bootleggers, and customers streamed through the house at all hours of the day and night. This was what Carmen Porco was born into; these were his roots.

The bungalow where Babe spent his early childhood had a front porch, living room, small dining room and kitchen, and three bedrooms and one bathroom upstairs. Daisy and Carmine slept in one bedroom; Babe's oldest brother, Jojo, slept in another; and Babe and Anthony, whom everyone called Cheech, and who was the closest in age to Babe, slept in the third.

Babe's second-oldest brother, Pat, was married and living up the street by the time Carmen could walk. Babe's grandmother, Genevieve, whom he called Nana, slept in an extra space that led to the attic. Genevieve helped take care of the kids and Jojo while Babe's parents worked the business.

The bungalow was rundown and mostly ordinary. At times you could hear water leaking in the attic or rats playing in the basement. But there was one special feature in the house: a great big potbellied stove. It was huge and took up most of the living room.

"We had eight chairs around it, plus lots of room to sit on the floor. There were always people coming in and out. Sometimes they played cards on the floor. Some people came to the front door, some came through the kitchen at the back, but everyone gravitated toward the stove. We all called it Big Bertha," says Carmen.

Babe formed some of his earliest and most vivid memories around this stove.

"The adults would stoke Big Bertha up red-hot with coal and wood and sit around it talking, debating, or sometimes just being quiet," Carmen recalls. "Customers would come in, unbutton their coats, and put their boots up on the stove's iron railing to get some warmth. Even in the summer, when the stove wasn't burning, people gathered around it to tell stories, day and night."

The potbellied stove, the center of the house, made the Porco home a place of communion, warmth, and laughter. It was the place to be if you were poor and needed a drink. If you lived in Weirton during the late 1940s and early 1950s and wanted liquor, chances are that you bought it from the Porco family.

"We were like a lot of other Italian families, always gathering to eat and talk with immediate and extended family. But sitting around Big Bertha, I met all kinds of people, people who were different from us," explains Carmen. "I was blessed to be in a house where so many kinds of people came through the door, even before I was of an age to understand how skin color was used to define a group of people and to separate them.

"I don't remember anyone ever arguing on Division Street. Later, after we opened the tavern, there was more space and people tended to get into arguments—but around that potbellied stove, life was always peaceful."

It was also very hectic, and everyone was required to pitch in and help, especially after Carmine developed a bad case of emphysema after years of working in the coal mines and the mill. By the time Babe was seven or eight, his family's house on Division Street was a fully operational "house of liquor and booze," as he recalls. The air in the house smelled of alcohol.

Even at a young age, Babe pitched in, sweeping up and entertaining customers—or letting them entertain him—while his mom or dad filled orders. When the business was still mostly in bootlegging, customers brought their own jugs to fill, and his father or mother went to their basement to get the wine. Carmen remembers that the basement housed his father's huge wine press and that a string of wine barrels rested along one wall.

Business didn't stop even when the Porcos went to bed. At any given moment, there might come a knock at the door. "I never heard either of my parents complain about a customer coming at a bad time," Carmen recalled. "As far as my father was concerned, there was no such thing as regular hours." Babe was a light sleeper, and when a knock came in the middle of the night and his mother got up to fill an order, he worried about her. "I had dreams of becoming her hero if something bad happened," he recalled from his early days, "but there was never so much as a raised voice during one of those midnight visits. Everyone was always respectful."

Still, as a youngster, Babe knew that his mother took on heavy burdens. She had Jojo and her two youngest to take care of in addition to the family business, where she was often wholly in charge when Carmine's physical limitations prevented him from working. Also, when the steel mill laid people off, she helped rally support for neighboring families.

"I was always impressed by my mother's stamina," says Carmen. "She never complained or thought of her own needs, but she always said to me, 'When God shuts a door, he opens a window.' As a kid I didn't know what that meant, but I do now. She had an iron will, but she always focused outward." Carmen credits his mother for giving him that same outward focus.

While Daisy was steadfast in her focus on others, his father Carmine believed that he needed to exude hardness and strength at all times to deal with life on the North Side. This hardness, though, was not cynical. Carmine had a deeply rooted sense of justice, though often articulated through anger. Babe often felt the brunt of that anger and thought his dad favored his other brothers over him.

CHAPTER TWO

Brothers

Jojo

BABE'S OLDEST BROTHER, JOJO, HAD DOWN SYNDROME and did not speak. When he was young, Carmen had a hard time understanding his brother Jojo. "I didn't understand the shape of his face and head, or why his tongue always stuck out a little. I remember my mother and brother Pat trying to explain to me what it meant to be born with Down syndrome and, in Jojo's case, why he couldn't talk."

What was clear to Babe was that his oldest brother was gentle and kind: "He would tickle me and make me giggle, and he was always helpful with customers. He had one sound he'd make to greet people or say good-bye: '*Momo.*' People always seemed to understand him."

"Jojo was a character," adds Carmen. "He was the only guy who could go up to another man's wife and make a noise that meant he wanted to dance. He couldn't talk, but he could dance. And the women danced with him like you wouldn't believe."

Later, when Babe was older, Jojo would take him downtown on Sundays. Jojo could navigate the busy streets and negotiate the bus, and people in the community looked out for him. The brothers would stop at bars and restaurants, and people would give them free sodas and candy bars, and then they'd go to the movies, where the theater owner would often give them free popcorn.

"Sometimes Jojo liked to watch the movie twice," Carmen recalls. "I didn't understand why he would watch it again, but he enjoyed himself all the same."

Jojo liked riding in cars as much as he liked watching movies. The Porco family didn't have a car, but Babe's Aunt Virginia would come and take Jojo and Carmen for rides in her convertible on Sundays. These rides made Jojo as happy as Carmen had ever seen him. Eventually, though, when their aunt was busy with her kids, the rides became few and far between. One Sunday, Jojo started making sounds and hand gestures to communicate with Carmen, and eventually Carmen realized that his brother was asking to go for a ride. Carmen couldn't bear to disappoint his brother, so he went out and stole an Oldsmobile 442.

"I took Jojo for a long joyride," recalls Carmen, "then dropped him off and parked the car a few blocks from where I'd stolen it. I felt like my brother's hero."

"We had a ball that day," he adds.

With Jojo, Carmen had a relationship that was more than loyalty, or fear, or even mutual respect. Jojo radiated a kind of love that inspired compassion in almost everyone who interacted with him. Jojo was an excellent checkers player, and he used to beat Carmen regularly. Even later in life, Jojo would ask Carmen if they could play checkers, and he would laugh when he beat him. "He was always the first to put a hand on you if you seemed scared or sad. He always seemed to take care of people more than they took care of him. In some ways, he was smarter than I was. He had a very sharp intuition about people," Carmen recalls.

One Saturday night at about 10:30 p.m., he and Jojo were helping out in their parents' barroom. A man entered, and almost immediately

Jojo made a gesture to Babe that meant, "Don't serve this guy. Get him out of here."

Right away, the guy said something to another man's wife; she walked away, but the husband noticed. Then the man ordered a double-double, which cost 75 cents, telling Babe to put it on his tab. "You don't have a tab here," said Babe, and the man started to get angry. He told Babe again to start a tab, but Babe refused. He went to take the man's drink back, but the man grabbed for it and it spilled.

At this point, Babe was standing in the middle of the Porcos' very long bar. Carmine kept double-barreled shotguns at either end of the bar in case of trouble, and there was a .38 revolver in the middle. Babe pulled the revolver on the man and told him to get out. "You've got 10 seconds to hit the door!" Babe yelled to the man when he protested. He cocked the hammer. But the man moved slowly. Babe wasn't sure if the man had a gun, and he was scared, so he went ahead and fired. The bullet missed the man and hit the doorframe as the man dashed for the exit.

"I could have been in much deeper trouble if Jojo hadn't alerted me," says Carmen. "I was only near that .38 because I knew to be wary. Otherwise, I would have been much farther away." Indeed, Jojo taught Carmen many lessons.

Carmen saw the ways that Jojo expressed his compassion and the ways that the community watched out for him. One day, a customer made a nasty comment about Jojo's appearance, how his tongue stayed partway outside of his lips. The other barroom regulars, who wouldn't stand for anyone talking about Jojo that way, dragged the guy out of the bar and beat him.

Jojo watched out for people, and they respected him in return. This left a big impression on Carmen, and he would model it later as the leader of a street gang.

Cheech

Although they were the closest in age, Babe didn't have a strong connection to his brother Anthony, whom everyone called Cheech. They shared a bedroom, until Babe was about seven years old. Babe tended to stay close to home, whereas Cheech often left in the morning and didn't return until dark.

"I loved to be home," says Carmen about the early days on Division Street, "talking and laughing with people around the stove. I didn't get to know Cheech very well until I started to leave the house more."

When Babe was eight years old, the family moved to a home in Weirton on Avenue B and built a new bar—Porco's Tavern—right next to the house. Carmen recalls that his dad was a big believer in cheap labor, so he tapped his sons to help with the construction.

"He taught us on the job," says Carmen. "We did everything ourselves."

He and Cheech would play in the dirt basement of the new bar until their father called for them to help, and then they'd carry lumber or bricks or do whatever was needed. Once, as he and Cheech struggled to hoist an 18-inch pylon into place, Babe realized for the first time that his brother was a hard worker but had a different temperament than his own.

"Cheech was a kind kid," says Carmen. "He didn't have any meanness of the streets in him, the way I did when I got a little older. Somehow he avoided it. I used to call him names, *wuss* or *pussy*, because although he was bigger than I was, taller and broader in the shoulders, he was always scared, and other kids pushed him around. Sometimes I tried to defend him, but then it would make me angry when he wouldn't fight back. If someone picked on him, he'd just cry and run home."

All this changed on a winter Saturday after the family moved to the Avenue B house. Babe was in the bar when a customer came in and reported that Cheech had been jumped by a bunch of kids just up the street. "They're beating the hell out of your brother," the customer told Babe, "and Cheech is taking it."

Babe acted fast. He sped through the door and up the street and decked a couple of the kids. Then he dragged Cheech home. Once they were there, Babe's anger at the kids turned to anger at his brother for letting it happen. "I wanted to convince him to fight back, but something he said about being reluctant to fight turned a switch inside me on, and we started fighting."

The brothers brawled in the house, knocking over furniture and breaking a leg on the China cabinet; they pushed and hit each other until Cheech threw Babe through a plate glass door, out onto the street. A sliver of glass went straight through the bottom of Babe's foot. Cheech told him to stay down and shouted, "I'm in charge now!" Cheech stormed up the street, going from house to house looking for the kids who'd just beaten him up, and threatened them. When he came back, Daisy was applying fatback to Babe's cut and Cheech reminded him of what he'd said earlier: "Don't forget who's in charge now."

Cheech was no longer the neighborhood wuss—now he was a fighter, like his brother.

And he fought with his brother often. Sometimes they threw punches at each other, but usually they would just try to figuratively beat the other one up by being better than the other at repairing cars. They each strove to make their own way and to prove themselves. Cheech began fixing cars and also worked in the mill. He was a dedicated worker, and eventually he became such a skilled and knowledgeable pipefitter that the mill practically couldn't run without him.

The cars Cheech restored ended up winning some of the largest car shows in the country, and he gained a reputation for the quality and level of detail in his work. He was very loyal to his family and lived his entire life in Weirton, within miles of the place they grew up.

Pat

Though Pat (John) was 20 years older than Babe and had moved out of the house by the time Babe was old enough to interact with him, Pat was in some ways Babe's closest ally.

"Cheech didn't like to go to Pat's house," Carmen recalls, "but I loved to because Pat's kids, Michael and Theresa, were about my age. Pat encouraged me to hang out with his family so I could play and have a normal life instead of being in the barroom all the time."

Carmen remembers one Christmas when he, Michael, and Pat built a model train together—not just the kind that circles the foot of a Christmas tree, but a full village with several locomotives on a giant sheet of plywood. This entertained the boys for hours. Pat was a pipe smoker, and at an early age Babe would pick a pipe from Pat's rack and hold it in his mouth as if he were smoking, imitating his older brother. Babe wouldn't become a pipe smoker for real until he was 15.

Pat was never content to take what the world gave him; he was always busy building the community he wanted. Pat had channeled the same dedicated work ethic Babe had seen in his parents into efforts at building his family and the community around him. For example, Pat started a Termite Baseball League in Weirton. Somehow, Pat convinced a local Italian entrepreneur named Mike Starvaggi, who owned a bus company and trucks and coal mine operations, to donate fields for baseball diamonds. The first field had about 10 diamonds on it; later, after selling the land to a developer, Starvaggi donated new land for the league, close by on the Pennsylvania border. He brought in a bulldozer to level it. With Babe's help, Pat built cement block dugouts and back-stops, and they installed electric lights.

"Pat was a gem," Carmen says. "He taught me everything I know about running wires." Carmen remembers one late night when he was helping Pat run electricity into the new barroom and it started to snow heavily. "The snow was coming down in blankets," Carmen says. "We heard a loud noise and went outside to find a tractor-trailer struggling up the grade of US-22, which ran along one side of the bar. As we watched, the tractor-trailer lost the battle and jackknifed. There was nothing we could do but watch, and soon our hands were going numb in the freezing cold. So Pat patched a hotwire to a little space heater outside to warm us up without missing anything. Then he brought out a Coca-Cola for me and a coffee for himself. It was past midnight, and here we were out in this shell of a building during a snowstorm, wiring the electric and just hanging out."

When he was in his mid-40s, Pat ran for alderman. "I was so impressed to think that a member of my family might reach for those upper echelons of power," says Carmen. "I was so proud."

Pat was Carmen's idol. He always found time to carve out little neat memories that gave Babe hope for what life could be. Pat's world was, in many ways, everything that the Porcos' barroom of Babe's young life wasn't. It was calm, safe, and warm—even on a cold, snowy night. Pat's kindness in making time for Babe awakened in Babe a yearning for a different life—one that was hopeful and just; a lifestyle that Carmen would someday help provide for others.

Relatives

Of the relatives who lived nearby, his mother's niece, whom he called Aunt Virginia, was always Babe's favorite. Virginia's mother had died young, leaving Daisy to help raise Virginia and her sister Mary. Virginia was married to Ambrose Bettino, who owned Bettino's Market, a big store stocked with groceries, appliances, and haberdashery. They lived in a wealthier part of town, Weirton Heights, not far from Babe's family's original home on Division Street in distance, but a world apart in other ways.

"Their house was like a mansion to me," reminisces Carmen. "When you walked on their deep pile carpet, your feet sank into it. It seemed like they had everything."

Virginia was soft-spoken and beautiful. She drove a shiny two-door fastback Oldsmobile, a car that Babe loved. She used to let him sit in the driver's seat and pretend to drive. He recalls that she was never cross with him or strict about him not getting the car messy even when they went for ice cream. "Babe," she would say to him, "you're the twinkle in my eye." "That sure made me feel special," Carmen remembers.

Donald Ambrose and Virginia's son, was the complete opposite of his parents. "Donald seemed to have everything and not appreciate what his mom and dad provided for him," Carmen says. "He would often let us know that he was better than us. Aunt Virginia would give us some of his clothes that he no longer liked or had outgrown. And they were nice threads. Donald would try to belittle me when we ran into each other at the high school—he was a senior and I was a sophomore—'Oh, those look good on me, but they don't look good on you.' Then everyone would know that they were hand-me-downs. He relished the idea that he was successful and up there. I never felt that he appreciated the hard work that his mom and dad did to get them there. I considered him to be spoiled."

Starting when he was eight, Babe stocked shelves and swept floors for Ambrose at Bettino's Market; eventually he graduated to sectioning and butchering sides of meat. One year, the person Ambrose usually hired to decorate the store's large display windows for Christmas fell ill and couldn't do the job, so Babe volunteered. Although he was still in grade school, he took the job seriously, and to Ambrose's delight, the displays ended up looking great. So he gave Babe more responsibility.

Ambrose owned a Christmas tree lot, and he made Babe a deal. He knew how much he needed to make on each tree to turn a profit, but he told Babe he could pocket the difference if he wanted to try to sell them for more. The bargain came with a warning, something Ambrose said often: "Never try to make a quarter off someone you might lose. Instead, make a nickel off someone who's going to come back time and again."

Babe didn't heed the warning. The first Christmas he worked for Ambrose at the tree lot, he pocketed over $700. "You're doing it wrong," said Ambrose, which Babe didn't understand. How could he be doing it wrong when he'd made so much money? "Let's just see how many customers come back next year," Ambrose declared.

Ambrose was right. Carmen confesses, "I must have lost him 30 percent of his customers. After that, the lesson stuck."

Also residing in Weirton were Babe's cousin Mary, Virginia's sister, and her sons, Rudy, Vince, and Tojo Bruno. Rudy Bruno, Babe's cousin, drove a sharp, beautiful convertible. As a young boy, Babe helped Rudy wash his car in exchange for a ride and a hot fudge sundae. By the time he was 13 or so, Babe would hang out at the Ethel gas station, where Rudy ran the business, and Rudy would teach him how to take apart and put together an engine. Babe's love of cars grew. By the time he was 13, he'd seen enough as a passenger to know he wanted to sit at the wheel, and Ambrose would let him do some delivering for Bettino's in Ambrose's brand-new F-150 pickup. "When I passed a cop," Carmen recalls, "I just sat up real straight."

Neighborhood

In many ways, the North Side of Weirton appeared to resemble the Greenbush neighborhood of Madison, Wisconsin, before it was dissolved by urban renewal in the early 1960s. In the Greenbush neighborhood, black, Italian, and Jewish families lived in the same neighborhood, and there was a level of harmony that existed between the different racial and cultural groups. The same kind of harmony existed in the North Side in Weirton, although the residents also had their problems.

"There were racial dividing lines," Carmen says. "There were segments in the Italian community who said, 'Hey, we're the same as black people because we are oppressed too. We're not considered Anglo-Saxon.' There were others who said, 'To hell with it. I'm getting better.' And they would move up and out. Within our family, some looked down on us because we stayed in the African-American community."

But overall Carmen felt his neighbors had much more in common than their differences. "It was a chaotic kind of peace. We were a mass of people who all looked different," recalls Carmen, "but somehow the differences didn't matter back then."

"Instead of being divided by race, we were united by poverty," Carmen adds. "The community stuck together, united by several things. We all enjoyed good food, and music, and community; and also we were all poor, all outside of mainstream society. We felt less black or Italian than unwanted, in other words."

Winters could be harsh. In 1952, when Babe was just five years old, it snowed so hard that his brother Pat shoveled a path through the snow with walls higher than Pat's head. Down by the mill where the Porco family lived, Carmen says the blast furnaces would turn snow different colors—dark orange and blue and green. The colors were a product of the milling process, and the result was toxic.

"We couldn't eat the snow because we'd get a mouth full of graphite," Carmen explains.

When the weather broke each spring, the Porcos and their neighbors started spending more time outside, planting flowers and gardens and helping each other out. And the families held impromptu block parties and barbecues with hot dogs and baked beans, with kids sitting on the curb on blankets and someone's radio turned up loud and blaring music out of the windows of a nearby house. The kids would make a ball from whatever was on hand—"rag ball," Carmen calls it—and use a stick for a bat, and some grownups would pitch while the kids did the running.

Although Carmen fondly recalls warm moments like this about his old neighborhood, the world generally looked like a hard place from the bungalow on Division Street where he spent his early childhood. It was easy to see the divisions in the world around him between rich and poor, white and black. The distressing haze of oppression that the steel mill seemed to belch out often made it difficult for Babe to appreciate the community that supported him. It took time for the communal bonds that worked across Weirton's north side to become apparent to Carmen even though they radiated out from his parents' barroom. He met all kinds of people in the barroom, who left a lasting impression on his life.

CHAPTER THREE

Lessons from the Barroom

———————————————

MANY OF CARMEN'S CHILDHOOD MEMORIES, GOOD AND bad, took place in the barroom. When Babe was six, he met Bubba Jennings, an African-American man in his 80s and a regular customer, who would become one of Babe's first influences and like a father figure to him. Bubba was "skinny as a rail," according to Carmen, and a tobacco chewer. He'd spit into a spittoon and tell stories about growing up on a plantation, moving to Weirton, and working at the mill. "Sometimes," recalls Carmen, "the other adults didn't have time for him, but he had me, a little kid, at his feet, hanging on to his every word. Bubba was so unique; he was like a mythical figure to me."

Bubba had a pet raccoon he wrapped around the back of his neck, and every so often the pet would inch down and take a drink from Bubba's glass, sometimes a rather large sip.

Bubba would talk mostly about how much he loved summer and nature. "Bubba would occasionally crash at our place in the winter," Carmen remembers. "He loved living in a shed with no heat, but the cold sometimes forced him inside."

Bubba was a spiritual man, and he and Carmen would take walks along the train tracks, taking in the natural world. For Bubba, everything had a deeper meaning.

Once when Carmen was about eight, he and Bubba were walking along the tracks to go fishing in the Ohio River. They were barefoot, as they almost always were, and Carmen stepped on a snake with his bare foot. The snake slithered away.

"I jumped and started running," Carmen exclaims, snake-scare energy vibrating afresh in his voice. "But Bubba called me back."

Bubba explained that if you step on a snake with the sole of your foot, that snake will end up crushing your soul unless you kill it.

Carmen wanted to run as far from the snake as he could get, but Bubba insisted otherwise.

They spent a good hour searching for the snake, digging through the ash coal that made up the bed of the railroad tracks, until they finally found it. Bubba reached into the coal, pulled the snake out, and whacked it over the rail of the track.

"That snake was good and dead," Carmen muses, "but Bubba said it wasn't enough."

Another train was due in about 20 minutes, so Bubba stretched the snake out on the rail, and they kept walking toward their fishing spot.

Carmen's eyes grow soft in the telling: "When we heard the train coming, Bubba said, 'Babe, your soul is safe now.'"

For years, Carmen would think about Bubba's stories and words. "I think he meant to teach me that the most precious thing we have is our soul, and whatever we need to do to save it, that's what we should do. I still think of Bubba every time I see a railroad track, but I try not to go digging for snakes."

Bubba lived to age 96, and Carmen was 18 years old when he died. They had been inseparable for much of Carmen's childhood, and he missed his friend deeply. For Bubba, nature was the source of his faith in something beyond himself. For Carmen, witnessing that faith sparked his own journey toward something bigger than himself.

———

When Babe was 13 years old, the family business shifted to a new bar and restaurant they built on US-22. This location was first known as Porco's Tavern and then renamed as Porco's Club so locals could buy memberships to drink legally on-site. Porco's Club lasted more than 40 years. The bar was open for business from 7 a.m. to 2 a.m. to attract workers coming off all three of the steel mill's shifts.

Babe worked in the barroom, cleaning spittoons, restocking coolers and shelves, and sweeping the floor. Eventually, he learned how to serve the customers, to listen to them, and to keep his eyes and ears open for trouble. Before Porco's was officially a legal club, Babe knew where to hide the liquor bottles in case the police stopped by. More often than not, Babe was still helping clean up an hour past closing and did not get to bed until 3 a.m.

Business varied, but when it was heavy, Daisy's mom and Babe's aunts would help out. The Porcos also had two employees, Queenie and Jeannie, who were treated more like family than employees and who stepped up their responsibilities when Carmine was sick or business was extra busy. But Daisy rarely asked for help. Carmen recalls Jeannie chastising Daisy for not asking her to come in earlier to help ease the load.

Carmen also remembers learning some important lessons from his dad:

Carmine would say things like, "Don't ever make one issue the whole relationship." "There was a guy who would come into the bar, and he and my dad would always end up fighting. The guy stabbed my dad once. My dad shot him once. Another time, the guy beat my dad up.

Then one day this guy comes in, and my dad had one booth that if you went there, it was the business booth, and they talked for a while. My dad said to me, "Go get my coat and hat." I'm wondering about where in the hell he was going; he was going out with this guy with whom he had always fought. It was a Saturday morning, and I was wondering what was up. I wanted to ask my dad, but he would have beaten me. They left, and it seemed an eternity before my dad came back. I wondered if the other guy was dead somewhere.

When my father gave me his coat and hat, I asked him why he went with that guy. He said, "Hang them up, and I'll tell you." Then he said, "The guy came to me and needed help. He needed someone to go with him while he turned himself in, put up the bail, and all of that. And that's what I did."

I asked him again, why he would do that. My father stood, looked up at the sky, and said, "You Americans. Don't you understand that if someone asks you for help, you don't say that you don't like that guy so you're not going to help? If you are able to help the person, you help them. You heard me, because I noticed you were listening. You heard me say that I was going to help him, but I didn't want him to think that I liked him."

But I said, "Yeah, but you went and helped him."

He said, "That's right. You have to help everyone you have the ability to help. It's not your right to say no."

The same man returned to the bar three Saturdays later. Carmen braced himself for trouble—a knife this time, maybe, or even a gun—but the man kept his tongue, and so did Carmine. They never came to blows again. Maybe helping people, no matter what, can change them, not just for a moment but forever. Years later, the man even spoke at Carmine's funeral.

Something else Carmen remembers from that bar before he was even 15—he lost his taste for alcohol. He credits his father for that. One day Carmine offered Babe a strong Italian cigar and filled a glass with his homemade red wine. He made Babe drink it until he couldn't drink anymore. Babe was sick for three days, and he never went near the stuff again. After that, he only drank RC Cola.

Queenie, their long-term employee, treated the barroom like a home and the Porcos, including Carmen, like family. Carmen remembers, "There were times when I was hurt, and maybe my mother was too busy to notice, but Queenie would get it out of me. She helped me discuss things I felt."

Once, Carmen was upset about a girl he liked who came from a well-off family: Why couldn't he have been born to a wealthier family? Why did he have to work in a bar and clean spittoons? Carmen is embarrassed to think of this now. Back then, Queenie said to him, "You think everything is rosy in that girl's family? It's not. Look at what you have instead of what you don't have." Queenie, among others, taught Carmen to see his barroom and neighborhood in a new light, and he began to count his blessings. A good number of the many blessings he found were the regular customers and community members who came to believe in Babe and show him through their actions the power of their faith.

During this reflective time, Carmen would think back to his old friend Bill Smith, who always said, "We all have the same Creator, Carmen. And we all bleed red." Or Bubba Jennings, who treated people and animals alike with unfailing gentleness and respect.

Another customer Carmen warmly remembers was Gene, an African American who earned a degree in architecture but couldn't get work. He was a dapper man, tidy and stylish in appearance, who spent his time in the bar sipping a drink and smoking a cigar in a holder and making sketches.

Because of Gene's skin color, no one gave him a chance, but when Carmine was building the bigger tavern, he hired Gene, and Gene came up with a plan to make sure the new floor was properly supported.

Gene was never sour about the cards he'd been dealt, recalls Carmen. "Once, he told me, 'Babe, you may leave this place to prepare yourself better, but remember this is where the treasure is.'" It would have been easy to cast off his life in the barroom, but Gene reminded Carmen to embrace his upbringing and to take it with him on the journey that would follow.

One day Carmen recalls a customer coming in visibly distraught. When the other men asked the customer what was wrong, he explained that his wife needed an operation and he didn't have the money. The barroom rallied to assist him. Within half an hour, the group of men on hand had raised $3,800. "But I can't pay this back," said the man, and the others told him he didn't have to.

In the barroom, there was a great diversity of people, not only in background but also in points of view. "The steel mill brought people from Israel, Pakistan, Greece, Japan, and here were all these different philosophies of life and religion," describes Carmen. "Sitting around one game of checkers or chess or cards, someone from Saudi Arabia might be playing with an African-American man and a white man and a Greek man and an Italian man. They'd all be playing or watching and making suggestions. It was a motley opinionated crew." Sometimes, these disagreements broke out into fights, but more often people just talked and argued their points of view.

Carmen absorbed the generosity of spirit and resources from these experiences, inside the barroom and outside of it, but he also absorbed a message about equality, since the recipients of service and the people offering service were of all colors and ethnicities. The thing that united them was their neighborhood and their circumstances, and these things were stronger than any divisions sown by skin color.

"No one in the barroom ever forgot each other's humanity, even when they got into fights," Carmen remembers. "The barroom taught me that our worth is dependent on connecting and treating each other as interdependent humans with dignity."

The Porcos' barroom was, Carmen sees now, a laboratory of theology, psychology, and sociology. The coat-tailing of social status and economics and social networking that he would learn from the world in graduate school and beyond was never as real to him as that original incubator where he formed his earliest beliefs and passions. There, in the bar, life was boiled down to one dominant fact: All people, regardless of income, have dignity and worth.

Carmen also recalls the fun side of the barroom. It was jam-packed on Fridays with all types of people in a smoke-hazed, dimly lit space; the jukebox blasting, everybody dancing, the liquor pouring, and people on Weirton's North Side leaving their troubles at the door.

CHAPTER FOUR

Bobo Young

ABOUT HALFWAY THROUGH THIRD GRADE, WHEN HE WAS eight years old, Babe became best buddies with a smart, mischievous, and wise-beyond-his-years African-American boy named Bobo Young.

"I never knew his real name—no one exchanged full names back then—but it didn't matter. I liked Bobo right away because he was always getting into trouble with the teacher, which otherwise was my job. Finally, I had some company!" laughs Carmen.

Carmen recalls how segregated his classes were in his early school years: "Poor kids were put in the back of the room, and the other kids were seated alphabetically. We didn't get any input; we were never called on. There was a belief that poor people were poor because they couldn't think. Being poor was considered a character flaw."

By the fifth grade, Carmen was fed up with the seating and the way that he and the other poor kids were treated. He was determined to do something about it.

"My dad said, 'Don't go looking for trouble,'" Carmen recalls, "'but if it comes your way, do something about it.' That motivated me. At the end of fourth grade, during the summer, I told my dad that I was going to cause trouble because I wanted to be seated alphabetically. He understood what that was all about. He said, 'You do what's right, and I will back you.'"

Shortly thereafter, Babe walked into the classroom one morning and sat next to the girl whose name alphabetically came right before his. The teacher immediately sent him to the principal's office, where he was subsequently expelled.

His parents backed him up and got Carmen reinstated in his class. The school changed its policy to allow kids to sit wherever they wanted. They could even sit together by race, class, or gender if they chose to do so. But the end result wasn't exactly what Carmen had anticipated, because many of the poor kids chose to stay sitting in the back of the room.

"I asked Bobo, 'Why are you sitting back here? Why don't we sit alphabetically or sit in the front?' He said, 'No, we won the battle, and now it's our choice to stay where we are at.' I was delighted to know that I had jumped in and dealt with that issue and it had made a difference. But the free choice of people who have been oppressed sometimes is to stay in the same behavior mode. That has stuck with me all my life to wonder why people take on the victimization of the oppressor," Carmen recounts.

Babe and Bobo loved to play street football and thought they were the greatest players on the earth.

"We were somewhat foolish because we didn't need a grass field to tackle somebody—if they went out of bounds on the sidewalk, we'd hit 'em," Carmen says. "We'd challenge each other, like 'I bet you can't go up that tree and jump off.' We did crazy stuff!"

Bobo and Babe were kindred spirits. Through that early friendship, Carmen learned that poverty is a great equalizer. It allowed the two to overcome any perceived difference that served as a barrier to their relationship.

"Not having money causes people to think alike, to become bitter and think they're not good enough," Carmen says. "If we were good, we'd have things, so we believed something was wrong with us. The hopelessness in that neighborhood wore all of us down."

In the early days, Babe and Bobo cemented their friendship by meeting at the mill gate at the bottom of Avenue B, where they would sit on soda crates and watch women walk by, making wisecracks and comments that would get them into trouble. Once a mother went by and heard them talk about her, and the next day the two boys caught hell when their families got wind of it.

"We both got our asses whipped," recalls Carmen, laughing. "One of life's many lessons is that people have value beyond what you can see." That lesson was beaten into Carmen time and again, even while it seemed the whole world was made to devalue him and his friends.

The two boys loved to goof off together and make each other laugh. But Bobo also had a mature, serious side.

"Bobo had a confidence and peace about him that none of the other kids had, including me," Carmen says. "He was one of the few people I really trusted. He had a moral compass I didn't have, though we goofed off like you wouldn't believe and we did the most dangerous things together."

For example, Babe and Bobo made their own wooden bikes with no brakes, which they called Hinky Dinks, and soared from the top of Avenue B down into traffic, nearly killing themselves in the process. Carmen says they were always taking risks.

"Bobo and I could just look at each other and know exactly what the other was going to do," Carmen says. "Once, we were walking by this market, and outside there was a bin of the most delicious looking apples. Bobo looked at me and I looked at him, and we grabbed two in each hand and took off."

Bobo and Babe made their own rules. In a world that seemed hell-bent on putting them in their place, they fought back to make their own space. Sometimes Babe fought for constructive goals, like sitting wherever he wanted in class; on the flip side, however, he was getting more aggressive and violent as he spent more time hanging out on the streets. That included running around with a gang.

"It all started innocently enough," recalls Carmen. "We were just a bunch of kids who hung out together, at school or at the Cove, the business district down in the valley. But after a while we realized that the more we hung together, the more protected we were. We were known as *Those Kids*, the bad kids. This gave us a gang-like reputation."

"A turning point came one afternoon when my mother asked me to go to the corner store to pick up some Tabasco sauce for the barroom," Carmen recalls. "She gave me $10 and asked me to go down to Gus's, the local grocer. Down at Gus's, I was confronted by some other kids who had their own little gang. I had the $10 in my hand, so they decided to beat me up and take the money."

One kid, about 12 years old, cut Babe's arm with a knife.

"I was like a baby," Carmen recounts. "After I took my beating, I went home crying. My mother asked me what was wrong, and when I told her, she started whacking me with a broomstick, telling me to be a man and not let people push me around. She actually broke the broom, hitting me with it. Damn, it hurt."

After this second beating, Babe went down to the basement to be alone. He knew he wasn't going to find any peace, inside the house or outside of it, without a plan of action.

"I decided, from that day on, that I was going to be a gang leader," Carmen says. "I knew that I needed to generate fear in others. Fear of me!"

Resolute, he took a piece of hickory wood about 10 inches long and affixed a nail to the end. He ground the nail until it was sharp. Then he practiced using it as a weapon.

"I went back out onto the street, and those fools came after me again," Carmen recounts.

Babe took aim for the older boy who'd cut his arm, and got him between the thumb and forefinger with his makeshift weapon.

"That boy never held a knife or a gun to me again," says Carmen.

Word traveled fast. From then on, Babe was the new "bad boy" on the block. "I let it be known that it was either my way or the high-way," Carmen remembers. "If I had showed any weakness, I would not have made it. This was my way of surviving. So by the time I was 10 or so, I was deep into something that I thought I was controlling—when in fact it was controlling me."

After that incident, Babe made the rules for the other kids, and to his surprise, they followed. By 11, he was the leader of a neighborhood gang. There were about 12 kids in the group, including Bobo Young. They got into fights—over rumors and girls, mostly—and hot-wired cars and broke store windows. "If it wasn't tied down, we'd steal it," recalls Carmen.

Back then, street gangs didn't have fancy names and didn't market themselves on the street.

"We didn't want to be known," Carmen says. "We were just a group of kids who hung out together, and unfortunately we made bad decisions. We did such stupid things. We got into fights, did pranks, stole, and then sold the stuff we stole."

Babe's gang also ran what he calls a "protection racket," where they terrorized local merchants—Gus's grocery store, People's Restaurant, Tony's Confectionery, and the local bars—into forking over $5 per month to keep Babe's gang on their good side.

"If they didn't pay, we'd bust up their place and disrupt the customers or break the windows or throw things on the floor, all kinds of stupid stuff," describes Carmen. "They'd call my parents, but I usually was able to weasel my way out of it. I'd blame the other kids, for one thing."

The gang also dealt with other kids who bothered or stole from the merchants.

"Five bucks per merchant was big money for kids in the '50s," says Carmen. "I think something people in the town realized was that if they tried to stop us, we might get even worse."

As for the police, the family business came in handy during Babe's most troubled years. Porco's Tavern was in a dry state, so the local cops knew the place and the Porco family quite well. According to Babe, the cops would come by regularly to get paid off. When his dad was sick, Babe was the one to hand over an envelope full of cash.

Carmen vividly remembers looking inside of the envelope once: "I figured out that by rank they got between $25 and $75 every month, plus a case of beer or jug of wine. I had evidence of what they were really up to and they knew me, so I wasn't too concerned about getting hauled in."

During this dangerous time of his youth, Carmen developed what he now calls his "gift of gab" —his ability to talk and persuade people. He not only learned how to be an effective speaker and leader on the streets, he could look at someone and intimidate them. It was his eyes that kept him at the top of the gang's leadership ranks.

"I could look at someone and not blink at all, and they'd know that their ass was grass—and I was the lawnmower," he recalls with a laugh. "It worked. People left me alone. They respected me out of fear, even if they didn't really like me. It felt great, for a while."

Although Bobo was Babe's best friend, there was another friend, John Ritter, who was known as John Dick, who also played a big role in Babe's life during this period. John Dick was one of the few other white kids in the neighborhood. His mother was diagnosed with cancer and fell ill when the boys were only 10 or 11 years old.

"We all felt bad for John because we knew his mother was going to die and he was affected greatly by it," remembers Carmen. "John was quieter and less interested in all of our nonsense, all the gang stuff and the stealing. He was just trying to survive and not get noticed. He and Bobo were my two closest friends. Bobo was always making me laugh my head off, but John showed me strength of character in the face of adversity."

Babe, Bobo, and John Dick used to go with a group, including an older African-American kid named Pop Simms, down to the Ohio River to fish. More than once, fishing turned into climbing a big tree and jumping into the water. Babe, who couldn't swim, was teased and goaded—until one afternoon he decided he didn't want to damage his reputation for toughness, and he went ahead and jumped into the water.

"I sank like a stone. I watched the bubbles go up and the rays of sunlight coming down through the water, and I didn't know what to do. I froze," says Carmen.

Pop Simms, who was 16 years old at the time, jumped in and pulled Babe up and swam him up to Brown's Island, the closest shoreline.

"He calmed me down and gave me some words of encouragement, then tried to convince me to swim back with him," says Carmen. "He said, 'Look, your choice is you can stay here overnight and the bears will get you, or you come with me and we can make it safely. I'll watch you. I'll be right by your side.'"

It was getting dark. Babe was scared, but he had no choice but to follow Pop back to the mainland. And he made it.

"It was a quick lesson in how to swim, I'll tell you that," acknowledges Carmen. "There was no reason for Pop to risk his own life, but he didn't hesitate. That moment left a strong impression on me, a sense of the essential equality of humans. When Pop Simms saved my life, it forever changed my impression of African-American people, because that was a very selfless act."

"He was not just getting me out of the water; he also took me over to Brown's Island," Carmen says. "It was about a quarter mile away from the mouth of the Ohio River. He talked to me and built my courage back up to jump in and swim across following him. It symbolized to me later in life the importance of our interdependence with one another, particularly with people who are different from us. Not only did I learn to swim, but I also learned a valuable lesson about a person who gives selflessly and then doesn't taunt you or call you chicken like the other kids."

When he got back to shore that day, Bobo and John Dick were waiting for him. They heard the train heading their way, so they hopped it for a ride back to the mill gate at the bottom of Avenue B.

"Bobo told me he was real glad I didn't drown," says Carmen. "I appreciated that."

Tragedy Strikes

Despite his close brush with death, Carmen did not yet appreciate the fragility of life and that the toughness and lack of fear he was working so hard to model would soon be shaken to its roots. Babe continued to lead his gang of kids in their petty extortion and fights and larceny for about three years, until he was going on 14. Then one night, his gang got into a fight with another gang over something trivial, a rumor or girl, something Carmen doesn't recall—and tragedy struck.

"Stupidity led up to it," he says. "Some group made a threat, and my gang decided to challenge it. We met up in a park and got to fighting."

When Carmen's gang approached the park, they did a lot of name-calling, as they'd always done. "Maybe there was a little spitting and threatening and taunting," he says, "that kind of thing. Other than a stick or a rock, we had never used real weapons before."

But all of a sudden, someone from the other group threw a rock—and that was it. Fight on!

"So my side went after them," Carmen says. "And they came right back for us. Then it was a brawl."

Carmen didn't see what happened, but when he heard sirens and the kids started to run away, he noticed that Bobo, his best friend and confidante, was still lying on the ground. He approached Bobo, urging his friend to get up—the police were on the way, they had to get out of there. But when he got close, he saw blood on Bobo's face.

Babe knelt beside Bobo and took his friend in his arms.

"I was too young to know that when a person is stabbed near the heart, that's it for him," Carmen says. "I figured Bobo would be taken to the hospital, that he'd be OK."

But Bobo knew he wasn't getting up again. As the rest of the kids fled and the sound of sirens wailed in the distance, Bobo's eyes came to focus on Babe's, and his mouth opened to speak. Babe leaned in so he could hear his friend's words.

Bobo's words struck Babe with the force of a punch to the gut.

"Babe, you've got to put a stop to all of this," Bobo pleaded. "You can get these guys off the streets. You can make a difference; you can make things right."

Nearby, car tires screeched as the police approached. Babe didn't know what to do. With his friend's words echoing in his mind, he gently laid Bobo on the ground, then took off running.

Bobo was taken to the hospital that night, but he was pronounced dead on arrival. His final words to Babe—"You can make this right"—were the last he ever uttered.

CHAPTER FIVE

Dave Stone

FOR DAYS AFTER BOBO'S DEATH, BABE COULDN'T EAT OR sleep. "There was no investigation," he recalls. "Just another poor boy dead. My best friend."

Babe was devastated by the loss and haunted by Bobo's final plea. Bobo's words cycled through his head, whether he was awake or sleeping. Babe looked at the world differently and reevaluated everything from that day forward, even his home and the tavern. In addition to the sadness he felt in losing Bobo, Babe was overwhelmed by guilt.

"I wondered if it was maybe all my fault that we'd gotten into the fight that night, if it should have been me stabbed instead of him. I can still close my eyes and feel what it was like to be there on the ground with Bobo, knowing I was partly to blame," he says.

Babe had seen his parents' toughness, and had endeavored to make himself as fearsome as they were. If someone hit him, he hit them back harder. But now the lifestyle of the streets that Babe had been living had resulted in the violent death of Bobo, and the tragedy left Babe feeling hopeless.

Babe knew he needed help to cope with the loss of his best friend, as well as to make changes in his life to respect Bobo's dying wish. He did not have a lot of people he felt he could confide in or even talk with, and none of his friends seemed as though they were ready to make different choices and change their futures. Babe searched for answers in the barroom, the patchwork community that surrounded him, and the family that had cared for him through all of his previous bad decisions.

He had yet to discover a faith in anything other than his own street gang code of might makes right, but now he desperately needed help. There was one person who might be able to help him: a pastor named Dave Stone who had been trying to reach Babe for some time now.

Babe first met Dave when he and his wife, Darlene, drove into the neighborhood in their red-and-white Nash Metropolitan wagon several years before. Dave was moving into Weirton to become the Men and Boys Director of the Weirton Christian Center, which was located just down the street from Porco's Tavern, on Avenue D parallel to the steel mill. Until this time in Babe's life, he'd considered the center a place for other kids—"good" kids—not kids like Babe and his friends, who were always getting into trouble. They hadn't felt welcomed at the center, but when Dave Stone arrived, all of that changed. Soon the center would be one point on the triangle that made up his childhood stomping grounds: his father's barroom, the steel mill, and the Weirton Christian Center.

"Dave was snow-white, not a pink pigment anywhere, and his wife, Darlene, was gorgeous and tan. We had never seen such a couple," Carmen remembers. "All of us guys stood around ogling the lady."

Shortly after his arrival, Dave approached Babe and his friends and asked why they were hanging out on the streets. They told Dave that they weren't allowed in the center.

"And he didn't ask what we'd done to get kicked out," Carmen says. "He just said, 'Why not? Was there a problem?'"

So this piqued Babe's curiosity, as it was one of the first times someone had asked "Why" instead of just reiterating that the center was not for them. He could see there was something different about Dave. So Babe and his friends went inside, all the while trading comments about Dave's wife. It was Darlene who interested most of the boys, not Dave. But Babe followed Dave to his office at the back of the building.

"Dave invited me in to talk," says Carmen, "and I told him he could be fired just for sitting down with me. He said, 'Look, I want to work with you guys, but I need some help.'

"My initial response was, here's a plump white boy from Minneapolis, spoon-fed, who knows nothing about people in poverty. This guy is college-educated but naive."

Despite their skepticism, Babe and his gang gave the Christian Center a try, and it began to change some of their lives and keep them off the streets. "We had Golden Glove boxing," Carmen recounts. "Some of the guys, who were on the street, found that as an avenue for them to find affirmation and acceptance." There was also wrestling and wood-working and model building. All of these activities allowed kids to accomplish something and be something. It gave them a sense of independent accomplishment.

Carmen adds, "Prior to that, we were all afraid of our own independence. Those activities Dave opened up at the center now became interest areas where each person had a sense of accomplishment. One of the kids made a table for his mother. He was very proud of the fact that he cut the wood. He sanded the wood. He glued it together. He stained and varnished it. It was a very prized thing for his mother. Another kid loved to detail model airplanes. It gave him a sense of being a pilot in the air force or something. All of a sudden, where there had been emptiness, now the center gave them activities where certain little things were significant to the kids because it was something that they did, something that they created, and it looked good.

"There was a collection of things that we had built: airplanes, battleships, and things like that. We raised money for the center by selling them. When someone bought one of those trinkets, as someone referred to them as, we were elated. And it was a way where we were giving back to the center. We were able to make that contribution.

"The Christian Center gave hanging out in the streets some real competition. There was the simple fact of acceptance; the doors of the center were open, and it had resources that allowed each kid to say, 'I'm interested in that.' One kid was just interested in weightlifting. He got to the point where he could dead lift over 200 pounds. Another kid was good at boxing, and they had competitions he could participate in. All of a sudden, some of the same activities they did in the street that was considered gang-oriented, when they did it in the center, it was considered good sport." Dave had made that all possible.

Dave would walk and talk with the boys, and he had a calming effect on Babe. He wanted to convert them—but they resisted. Remembers Carmen, "We'd say, 'Don't give us this religious crap. If God is so good, why are we so poor? Why does the steel mill get away with murder?'"

Dave told them that he didn't think it was God's design that they be poor, and he didn't know yet about the mill because he'd just arrived in Weirton.

"As he knew us better, he started to push the religion stuff harder, asking if we'd ever thought of giving our life to Christ. My sarcastic response was, 'Why doesn't Christ give his life for us?'" Carmen recalls.

"I challenged Dave about inequality," he adds, "and he reminded me that I'm white. I told him that was nonsense. I wasn't white, I was Italian. Then he explained that I was *Caucasian*—I'd never heard that word before. It was an academic term. We knew people as Italian, Irish, Jewish, and Black."

Carmen had never been baptized, but he'd been forced by his parents to go to catechism school every summer and also to do his duty as an altar boy during the year. He'd been skeptical of Catholicism at an early age. His parents weren't faithful practitioners, though they gave money to the church, and the most salient fact Carmen knew about religion was how the Catholic priest at the local parish treated him and his family—and it wasn't good. The Porco parents were nonpracticing Catholics because they didn't feel welcome, but their children went.

"I didn't even know what Lord and Savior meant. Dave used to sing that hymn, 'I have a joy, joy, joy, down in my heart,' and I would think, 'Does he not see the suffering around here?' I liked him, but he made me feel conflicted and angry, at least in the beginning," says Carmen.

One Friday evening, Babe and his friends were hanging around by the Christian Center, and Dave showed up. This particular evening, Babe felt Dave was trying to lay a claim on him—and he had an image to maintain. Dave persisted, and Babe felt crowded. He warned Dave to back off, told him to go back to his office and read the Bible, but Dave got closer still—so Babe hauled off and hit him in the jaw.

Dave fell back against a car. When he recovered, he said to Babe, "That hurt you more than it hurt me. You can even hit me again if you want." Then he reminded Babe of something that he's never forgotten. Dave said, "I don't like some of your behavior. But you are not your behavior."

"He was the first person who ever told me I wasn't a bad person," marvels Carmen. "That man scared the hell out of me because he acted in ways that people on the street didn't act. He challenged the fundamental core of my belief system."

A couple of days later, Babe waited all afternoon for Dave's Nash wagon to make its way down Avenue D toward the center, and when Dave drove up and got out of the car, Babe tried to be nice. After some small talk, Dave invited Babe inside to talk. Babe went inside and ended up crying like a baby and apologizing for hitting him. Dave had made Babe feel vulnerable as he started looking at himself through a new lens.

"I don't know what Dave saw in me, except that he knew I could lead and kids would follow," Carmen remembers. "I was impressed by the fact that he saw something better in me than I saw in myself. The center helped form me, because of him."

After Bobo's death, Babe poured out his heart and shared with Dave what his friend had said to him while he lay dying. Dave told Babe that this might be God's way of telling him something.

"In my heart I knew he was right," Carmen recalls. "I said to him, 'I think I need to give my life to Christ and do things differently. Is it too late for me?' Dave quickly responded, 'It's never too late.' We hugged and prayed together. His prayer was for God to help me move beyond my grief and lifestyle and find strength and wisdom."

The Calling

A few days after his meeting and prayer session with Dave, Babe had another dramatic incident that changed everything: he had an out-of-body experience.

He was asleep in his bedroom when he woke to find himself rising up from the bed; as he looked down on himself, a bright blue light illuminated his body.

When he returned to his body, he felt utterly changed and at peace. "I felt the strangest sense that I'd changed," he recalls. He woke for good later that morning, and the feeling of peace and certainty was still there. He went into the kitchen and found his mother. "There will be no more trouble from me," he said to her.

She was skeptical, saying, "Time will tell." Indeed it would, but Babe believed he had been transformed. The lessons of his life had been recast toward a new purpose; he had found a new faith.

It was a Saturday, which meant the Christian Center was hosting basketball games, so Babe went over there to find Dave Stone. He told him that God had called him to the ministry, and Dave looked at him with a huge grin on his face and said, "Glory Hallelujah!"

A few other churchgoers overheard what had happened and congratulated Babe. "I didn't feel the ground under my feet when I walked home that day," he recalls.

But not everyone in Babe's life was so happy for him. When he told his father what he'd decided, his father said, "Che cazzo," which means "what the fuck."

"You mean you want to be a priest, not a minister, right?" Carmine couldn't understand why his son would take up with a non-Catholic church, especially the Baptists, and it would be many years before he would come around to supporting Babe in his decision.

Dave took it upon himself to teach Babe about Baptist theology. To start, he gave Babe a Bible and asked him to learn the book and to be able to recite the chapters in order after church the following Sunday. Babe threw himself into the assignment. When the time came, he recited them in order and then added John 3:16: *For God so loved the world that he gave his one and only Son, that whoever believes in him shall not perish but have eternal life.*"

Dave reached into his drawer and pulled out a gold star, affixing it to the bulletin board. Babe felt like he'd earned a great reward. "What's next?" he asked.

"We're going to read the Bible cover to cover, together," said Dave.

After school from then on, Babe's life was radically different. His friends didn't understand why he kept hanging around with Dave. He liked to sit in Dave's office and talk to him, trying to understand his message about theology.

"I knew I wanted to continue having Dave's approval," he says, "because I looked up to him."

Babe already had a busy schedule. He'd come home from school, let his parents know he was safe, then head to his Uncle Ambrose's store by 4 p.m. to stock shelves and wait on customers until about 6 p.m. Next he'd go home and eat dinner and work in the bar until late—long after closing if his father's emphysema was acting up.

After he started working with Dave, and if his father was well enough, Babe would go straight to the center from his shift at Ambrose's store, then return home at about 8 p.m. and work in the bar.

"The days were long," Carmen recalls, but his new faith revitalized him.

Babe had committed to living the straight and narrow life, yet trouble still found him. Not long after Bobo's death, Babe was arrested, along with a few other friends. He hadn't done anything, but the police pulled him in just because they knew he was a troublemaker, or had been.

"The police were accusing me of things I wasn't involved in at all," he recounts. "They didn't think they could get me on the brawl and Bobo's death, but maybe wanted to nail me on some other stuff."

No one called Dave Stone down to the courthouse, but he showed up anyway.

"I was only behind bars for about an hour and a half," Carmen says.

Dave went to bat for Babe, and the judge agreed to release him to Dave's care, as long as Dave agreed to be responsible for him. If Babe got in trouble again, the judge told Dave, it would be Dave who got the blame.

"But Dave didn't blink. He had faith in me," says Carmen.

Babe expressed his gratitude to Dave by redoubling his efforts to study theology and sociology at the Christian Center, which had a robust library. He read the works of Emile Durkheim, Walter Rauschenbusch, and other theologians and philosophers. Some of these texts deepened Babe's understanding of social divisions and inequality. "It made me feel kind of weird," he recalls, laughing, "but I found it interesting."

With Dave's guidance, Babe started to think differently about his future. Before, he'd fantasized about applying to West Point and going into the military because that seemed the only way out of the life of working in the steel mill and the poverty that surrounded him. Now he started paying attention to politics, and though he wasn't allowed to watch political news, his father made an exception each time one of three men spoke: John F. Kennedy, Martin Luther King Jr., or Billy Graham. These were leaders—along with Dave Stone—that Babe was starting to realize could be role models for him.

Babe's life had taken on a new direction. He had become a Fundamentalist in which one translated the Bible literally and followed that literal translation blindly. Once you were born again, you were saved. And one believed that accepting Jesus Christ as his Lord and Savior would give him eternal life. Carmen didn't yet have a strong theological foundation, but he believed that if he did good, he would be saved.

"Later I would look at theology differently," he explains. "I moved from thinking one was saved by works to believing that we are given grace, saved or not saved. Eternal life could not be earned. It was granted through grace. What mattered was your intentionality of honor. The key element was whether you make a difference for other people."

But for now, Babe was delighted to be free of gang life and determined to make his way on a new path, thanks to Dave Stone.

CHAPTER SIX

From Barroom to Pulpit

―――――――――――――――――――――――――

BABE STILL WRESTLED WITH THE IDEA OF BECOMING A minister. He was taking his first steps toward learning Baptist theology, but his life was still rooted in the barroom. He struggled with the conflicts between life in the bar and on the street and a new life of faith and servanthood. Although life at the bar was hard, his family and community there lifted Babe up and helped him see things differently than society in general seemed to see them.

"My father always taught me not to think anyone who looks or talks differently is less than," Carmen explains. "He said, 'Don't ever think you're better than anybody. But don't let anybody ever convince you you're less than you are.'" Babe would find this piece of advice very timely when high school started that year.

Before Carmen's junior year, Weirton built a brand-new high school up in Weirton Heights, which was one of the better neighborhoods. Before that time, the high school was down in the valley, which was called the Cove.

"The Cove was like a neutral zone, where anyone could go. The Cove was the shopping strip, doctors' offices, bus station, and a movie theater, so we were there a lot," explains Carmen.

After the new high school was built, kids from the Cove—which was predominantly white—and kids from the North Side—which was predominantly African American, Jewish, and Italian—were bussed to the new high school, which was built in the campus style on a beautiful plot of land. Carmen was especially excited to learn the new high school had a planetarium, because he was interested in astronomy—he knew all of the constellations named for the Greek gods and all the legends about them. Carmen was a good student when he wanted to be.

His excitement was short-lived.

"We didn't get 10 feet onto the property that first day of school before a group of wealthy white kids came at us, pushing us and crowding us and calling us the N word," says Carmen. One of the white boys swung at Carmen, and Carmen swung back, knocking the kid out cold. Carmen started his year at the brand-new high school by getting called into the principal's office. Two of the three assistant principals of the school were white men who were ready to tar and feather him, as Carmen recalls, but one was an African-American man named Jim Wares. Jim had been a teacher at the segregated all-black "Dunbar School" before Weirton's schools were integrated. He was one of the few black teachers who kept their jobs during school desegregation.

On that fateful first high school day, Jim was the only adult who asked for Carmen's side of the story. Jim stood up for Carmen, even though it was apparent that they were in the minority and the majority had all the power at that new school. It was a lesson in group dynamics that Carmen would apply later during his housing management career: that even when you are outnumbered, you can wield ideas like justice, fairness, and equality against power and oppression.

"And thankfully," Carmen continues, "a fellow student—a white girl—spoke up and defended me. She told the administrators that the other kids had started it and I had just been defending myself." Carmen learned another important lesson that day: people are complicated, but very rarely are they either all good or all bad. He began to see that just as he was more than those who judged him thought, so, too, they could be more than just bullies or oppressors.

"Without her and Jim Wares there to speak up for me," Carmen concludes, "I would have been sent down a bad road on the first day at my new school."

Jim took Babe under his wing. He had heard from Dave Stone that Babe had a way with young people, so he set Babe up with a room for counseling other troubled students and mediating disputes. Initially, Jim was the only principal who sent kids to talk to Babe, but once the others saw how effective he was, they also started sending kids to him. Having headed up a gang, Carmen was used to giving other kids advice. Being a former gang leader also gave him street credibility. "Jim believed in me, and he gave me social affirmation. Jim was a beacon of light in that school. He made a big difference in my life," Carmen recounts appreciatively.

Soon after, Jim talked to the man in charge of the planetarium, Phillip Katril, who, after quizzing Carmen on his knowledge, gave Carmen a job running the planetarium on Sunday afternoons. This, combined with his work with Jim as a student leader, gave Carmen a new reputation. After six months or so, the bullying stopped.

"I beat the bully at his own game," recalls Carmen. While fighting with his fists had always gotten him in trouble, he was finding that defending himself by doing good had much better results. With Jim Wares' patient example and Dave Stone's faith in him, Carmen continued to develop a different outlook on life.

Carmen was excited for the opportunity to work in the planetarium, but his schedule was bursting. Every day he had school, work in the barroom and at his uncle's store, and volunteering with the Christian Center. Something had to give.

"The only thing I couldn't keep up with was my grades," recalls Carmen. Even so, he earned Cs without trying; if he'd had time to study, he might have done better, but his new life only added new responsibilities on top of those he already had to his family.

His family might not have supported his growing involvement in the Baptist community, or his preaching later on, but they did notice that he'd changed. He wasn't cursing or stealing or getting into trouble, and he was a regular and reliable part of the family business.

This nagged at Babe: "I wanted to honor my mother and father by helping in the barroom, but I felt like a hypocrite because we were selling booze, which was a sin and, in a dry state, was illegal to boot. Here I was serving every kind of booze you could imagine, and enjoying that because it was such a big part of my life—and at the same time I was asking people to give their souls to Christ."

Babe had begun reading the Bible with Dave Stone. He hadn't developed a deep understanding of the layered meanings of the scriptures yet. Carmen recalls, "I was a strong Fundamentalist at the time, interpreting the Bible literally. I took the scripture verbatim. But I never had the sense that taking Christ as your savior relieved you of your suffering. It was a sticking point for me. I was bothered by this part of my Fundamentalism, but I had nothing else to put in place of it." Over time, the lessons of the barroom would lead Carmen toward a social gospel, but early on he was torn between his Fundamentalist reading of the Lord's word and the lived experiences all around him.

Eventually, Babe would confess his feelings of conflict and guilt to a regular customer, an African-American man in his 40s named Bill Smith, who had long been a fixture at Porco's Tavern. "For whatever reasons, Bill and I clicked as if we were peers," recalls Carmen, "though he was 30 or 35 years older than I was."

Night after night, Bill would call Babe over to his table, tell the teenager to get himself a RC Cola and a Zagnut candy bar and to pour Bill a Canadian Club or Seagram's and Seven. Bill would sit quietly for a minute, then talk about whatever was on his mind.

Bill was, Carmen recalls, a "gentle soul" who, unlike the other tavern customers, never swore. He worked at the mill, never married, never knew his father, and lived with his mother. When Babe shared his guilt and conflict with Bill about serving alcohol while also dedicating his life to the church, Bill told him, "Look, I drink because I want to—you didn't pour it down my throat. People are going to drink no matter what."

Bill didn't like overhearing Carmine call Babe a "S.O.B." or "*stronzo*" (asshole), as Carmine sometimes did when he shouted at Babe in the barroom.

Once, Bill said to Babe, "You and I have a lot in common—we aren't sure we're wanted." Babe hadn't realized he felt that way until Bill put it into words for him. "That was hard for me," recalls Carmen. "I never asked my father why he was so brutal to me and never to my brothers. Maybe it's because he hadn't wanted me, but I don't know. I struggle with that to this day. The scars we cut early stick around forever."

That experience brought Babe closer to Bill, and he became eager to sit with Bill—eager to show, by listening, that Bill was both wanted and needed. To show that Bill was important to him. Years later this became a fundamental practice of Carmen's ministry—to listen to people and let them know that they are valued.

Once, Babe noticed that Bill was missing from Porco's Tavern two Saturdays in a row. When he returned, he ordered an RC Cola instead of a Canadian Club. Bill had been worried about his drinking for a long time, it turned out, and now it seemed he was ready to stop for good. He gave some of the credit to Babe. "You've been listening to me for a year," he said to Babe. "I realized that no one outside of me can heal what's inside." From that time on, the two drank sodas together as they talked.

Babe learned in his relationship with Bill that the most useful thing one can do sometimes is provide an ear. By just sitting and listening to Bill, Babe was also able to reflect on his own life. "The thing is," says Carmen, "it doesn't matter where you are. If you listen to people's hearts and do it sincerely, you give people the feeling that you're present with them, and even if you don't have the answer, you're companions in that moment. That's the best ministry."

Bill never expressed skepticism about Babe's newfound faith. He asked Babe, "Did you really feel God's calling?" And when Babe answered affirmatively, Bill said, "Great. Let's celebrate!" When it was time for Carmen to follow a path into the ministry, Bill didn't question him. "He said, 'You go for it!'" Carmen recalled.

Bill helped Babe see the world around him in new ways, and with that different outlook came different possibilities for the future.

The world can seem small when you are struggling to survive. The only place young Carmen wasn't regularly being told that he didn't belong was his own small corner of Weirton, West Virginia. But now he was beginning to explore new opportunities and realize that there was a larger world beyond the North Side of Weirton.

Carmen got a taste of the larger world through state politics around this time. George Tokash, a volunteer at the Christian Center and an English teacher at Carmen's school, ran for state assemblyman of their district the year Carmen was a junior. Tokash needed someone to help him carry the North Side, so he asked around for recommendations. Everyone at the Christian Center, as well as Jim Wares, told him the same thing: Carmen is your guy.

Carmen agreed to get the word out for Tokash's campaign and promised him that he'd carry the North Side by 90 percent. He didn't fulfill his promise—Tokash won the North Side by 87 percent. The night he won, Tokash called Carmen and invited him to be a page at the West Virginia capitol for two weeks. Carmen was thrilled and said yes immediately.

Carmen was 16 at the time. They left in Tokash's Chevy Corvair during a huge snowstorm, and the three-and-a-half-hour drive took more than six hours. As soon as they arrived, Carmen was given an orientation; then he spent his days on the floor of the state legislature, waiting for a light to go on that summoned him or another page to run an errand. In spending this focused time at the capitol, he got an intimate view of how politics worked, as well as how policies shaped the lives of the people back in Weirton.

Carmen didn't count on knowing anyone but Tokash during his two weeks at the capitol, but he ran into someone he knew from back home, a Hancock County sheriff named Joe Manypenny. Joe was one of the few law enforcement officers from Weirton who had never harassed him and had always given him good advice. He told Carmen to make sure to drop by his office at the capitol if he needed anything. Running into someone who'd known him, and seemed to approve of him both on the streets and in the state capital, gave Carmen the feeling that he was on the verge of leaving his past behind for good.

"When I told my friends on the streets that I'd found Jesus and was giving up the street life, they laughed," Carmen explains. "I was trying to convince them to give up the streets, and I was able to entice a few to get involved in the Christian Center, but the majority weren't interested. It was sad because I thought I could persuade them. I didn't realize what hopelessness does to a human being. Many of them continued to drift and got involved with alcohol and drugs. They stopped going to the center. Some fought in Vietnam. Some didn't return. Many died prematurely. I was saved in more ways than one."

He was now ready to leave the barroom for the pulpit.

CHAPTER SEVEN

Preaching the Gospel

BABE TOLD HIS DAD THAT HE WAS GOING TO PLAY BASKET-ball. He went as far as putting a basketball along with his shorts and tennis shoes in a gym bag. His father didn't suspect anything. "My baptism was a sneaky affair because my dad was against me becoming a Baptist because he was Catholic, so I had to come up with an alibi," Carmen explains. Gym bag in tow, Babe hustled down to the First Baptist Church of Weirton and was baptized by Rev. Archie Shawn on a Sunday morning.

"I felt jubilant about it because it was a journey I'd decided to make and I felt a serious sense of calling," Carmen recalls. "I wanted to dedicate my life to servanthood. When I was baptized, I felt it was complete, being dunked in the pool of water and the congregation witnessing it, and the words 'You're saved, in the name of Jesus Christ your Lord and Savior.' Those were powerful words to me . . . I felt cleansed and renewed and empowered, in faith and dedication, to do whatever I had to do to make it."

No one from Babe's family attended the baptism, and Dave Stone was out of town that Sunday, speaking, but Babe's secret didn't keep for long. Weirton is a small town, and word got out quickly. Babe's mother didn't mind much, but his father did. "He made it clear that he was Catholic and if I was going to be Baptist I needed to make it on my own," says Carmen.

Carmen already had an idea of life beyond the barroom, and he doubled his efforts to get out on his own. He used his knowledge of the Bible and his "gift of gab" to start preaching. He was convinced that if he was going to make his own way, it would be through religion.

When Dave taught Carmen about the Bible, his lessons were focused on conveying the dignity of the human being regardless of position or social status. He told Babe, "A fundamental thing that a servant of God must do is be blind and yet see the inner selves of the people." It was a lesson that aligned with Carmen's experience in the barroom, and it stuck.

By the time he turned 15, Babe was in the Baptist Youth Leadership program at the center. At that time, the American Baptists had 33 Christian Centers throughout the country. The ones with promising leaders were invited to attend a leadership camp and compete for a prize known as the Grand Sakima. The award involved knowing the Bible, surviving in nature, and leading a group in nonviolent action. Although Babe was only an average student, he figured Dave would teach him the Bible and he could handle the rest on his own. "I decided that I was going to win that prize," declares Carmen. Dave cautioned Babe to be realistic. It was only his first year, after all, and some kids had been competing for the Grand Sakima for a long while. Babe was insistent, and Dave nominated him for the award, which meant that Babe was headed to Indiana to participate in a national youth leadership conference.

Babe had only been outside of Weirton once, and that was to steal a car in Pittsburgh, 20 miles away. He had no sense of where the state of Indiana even was, but he saw the brochure for the camp where the conference would take place, Camp Okalona, and he thought it looked beautiful.

"I thought, 'Damn, I'm going to this thing, and I'm going to win this prize,'" says Carmen. To Dave, he said, "I'm going to win this, Big Boy."

"Soon he got tired of me boasting about how I was going to win this prize," Carmen admits, "but he never said anything about it. I'd never felt such confidence, even arrogance. This competition changed the whole complexion of Weirton for me—the place no longer looked like a dead end. I would be able to grow beyond the boundaries that had been put on me since I was very young." From many of Carmen's childhood friends, the way out of town was through the military, but for Carmen, the tracks that led him out of town were laid down in scripture. He became dedicated to learn more about not only the Bible but also social action.

The Christian Center collected many of Dr. Martin Luther King Jr.'s published works in the library and Babe began to read and study King's nonviolent philosophy. Part of winning the leadership prize involved making a speech and leading a mock protest. Participants also had to give a speech invoking the ideas of the gospel in the service of social justice, then show an understanding of nonviolent direct action.

"In other words, if someone spits on you, you don't jack them up. That was new for me," says Carmen.

Babe led the mock march at the camp, where others were instructed to spit on him to see how he'd handle it. He handled it nonviolently and with class. He gave the speech and sure enough, won the prize. He was ecstatic and couldn't wait to tell Dave and his parents.

Babe's mother Daisy was proud that he'd gone after something he wanted and made it happen. His father, though, kept admonishing Babe to drop his Baptist learning and get to work. Carmine was hard and reluctant to show any emotion. "I didn't know how proud he was of me until after he died," says Carmen. "I learned later that he'd been in a fight with a customer, and normally when that happened, he'd just take out his gun and shoot, but this time he'd let himself get badly beaten and ended up in the hospital. When my mother asked him why he hadn't shot the guy, he'd said, 'What would they think of Babe, who wants to be a minister, if his father kills somebody?' My father was a tough old bird and kept his feelings hidden. But when I heard that story after his death, I understood him a little better."

As for Dave, he was delighted at Babe's success at the leadership conference. He began pushing Babe to join him when he went on the road to speak at churches around West Virginia.

Although Carmen had known he had the ability to talk and persuade people, he hadn't realized how easily he could stand up in front of people and just let the words flow. Right out of the gate, Babe was determined to show that he could be a good Christian, that he could spread the word of Christ with his talents for speaking and persuading. He also helped Dave raise money for the center by speaking in churches.

The first church Dave took Babe to was in a Baptist stronghold. The First Baptist Church in Charleston, West Virginia, was one of the largest around, with 1,000 members in the congregation. Dave got up and made a few remarks, then introduced Babe.

Carmen remembers, "I got up there, and I started by saying that I wanted to talk about the Christian Center in the context of Jesus Christ and his teachings. Once I started talking, I started hearing the congregation get on board with me, saying 'Amen.'"

After the service, Dave and Babe went for dinner and celebrated with two hot fudge sundaes each. There would be other trips in other states, but that night Dave said the words Babe would remember for the rest of his life:

"Man, you're a better preacher than I am!"

"It gave me a high," recalls Carmen about speaking from the pulpit for the first time. "I was surprised at myself. Initially I was afraid. I'd never spoken before a group of people, particularly in a church—but after the very first time, when I got up and stepped into the pulpit, I felt no fear or reservations. I realized that no matter what, I had an opportunity to make a difference, inside Weirton and outside of it."

He knew then that he wanted to continue studying biblical scripture so he could speak on different themes. Dave obliged and taught him deeper interpretations of scripture.

Meanwhile, Reverend Shawn, the same minister who had baptized Babe at the First Baptist Church of Weirton, took on the role of teaching Babe how to be a more effective preacher.

"Archie was a darn good preacher. At the time, all I knew was that I liked to run my mouth. I knew we were created in the image of God, regardless of income or education or color, that there is one Creator and one world and one people. I felt this strongly. Archie talked to me about tone and atmosphere and delivery," recalls Carmen.

Soon after Reverend Shawn baptized Babe, he invited Babe to step into his pulpit and deliver a sermon. "The prospect of preaching at Archie's church was frightening," says Carmen. "I'd bought into the fundamentalism of faith and many of the Baptist principles, but standing at the pulpit and looking out into an audience of lay people was a different story. I felt inadequate. Here was a congregation full of adults—what could I share that they didn't already know? I assumed they were well-heeled in faith and well-versed in the Bible."

This was the moment when Carmen learned, early in his preaching career, never to grant the audience the assumption that they're superior to you in matters of faith, no matter your age.

He recounts, "I remember praying before I got up to speak, 'Lord, use me as your vessel; not what I've prepared but what you want me to speak to.'"

His prayer was answered because Babe didn't use what he'd prepared. Instead, he discovered a new voice, one with a tremendous excitement and energy for sharing the word of God.

"Everything just flowed," Carmen recalls, "and my feelings about faith and dedication and being called to serve all came together during my sermon on the essence of Christ, which is unconditional love. Later, I had a feeling that I hadn't said the things I'd said. I felt throughout the whole thing that my mind and my mouth were working and it was outside of me and I was just a vessel."

The congregation responded enthusiastically to Babe's sermon and his delivery, clapping and shouting "Amen!" and "Tell it like it is!"

"That was the day when I discovered I had something to say and was good at saying it," says Carmen, "and maybe I'd be a good preacher one day."

Around the same time, Babe also had the opportunity to preach to Reverend Highsmith's congregation at the African Methodist Episcopal (AME) Church. Reverend Highsmith was a different kind of pastor than the others in Babe's life—he knew most of the customers from the Porcos' barroom by name, and he visited his flock at home or in the street. Babe had attended his church on occasion and was always impressed by both his style of preaching and his pastoring outside the church. Reverend Highsmith went out, beyond his sermons, to minister to people.

"He met people where they were at," says Carmen. "His witness was quiet, yet profound."

When Reverend Highsmith heard that Babe had felt the calling to serve God, he asked Babe to take the pulpit at his church.

"I held Reverend Highsmith in extremely high regard, and when he invited me to speak to his congregation, I was overwhelmed," remembers Carmen. "'This is serious,' I thought. I was amazed that he would consider me adequate and capable to speak in his pulpit."

Babe ignored his own fear and accepted Highsmith's invitation.

"It's an experience I'll never forget. What a blessing it was to have someone in Weirton who had a profound dignity of faith and witnessed among the people without judgment. To be considered adequate to the task of speaking in his pulpit made me feel I was on top of the world," Carmen recalls. "I was no longer Babe the troublemaker. Now I was truly Carmen the preacher."

Jim Wares, one of the assistant principals at Weirton High School, had been in the congregation when Carmen had preached at the AME Church and remembered him well. After the service, Jim, who by this time used a wheelchair, had taken the time to go up to Carmen to let him know that he was impressed by his sermon. Carmen had, in a way, rewarded Jim's faith in him at the high school.

Carmen developed a good reputation for preaching during these engagements, but he wanted to do more. The West Virginia Baptist Convention leaders asked him to come to their summer camps to encourage young people. "I believed this was the right thing to do," says Carmen. "I would do an altar call, and 75 percent of the camp population would come down and give their lives to Christ. I sincerely enjoyed it. I was egotistical to think this was my power and influence."

Carmen was still digging for deeper meaning in the Bible. "I still didn't understand the Roman Empire or the parables. I was confused how Jesus Christ could act the way he did, because it's certainly not how I would have acted in his position. While I had grasped the more surface qualities of theology, I hadn't fully awakened to the underlying truths and spiritualism." This would become a lifelong quest for Carmen, to articulate what Jesus means in the everyday lives of people who are struggling with oppression.

He didn't have to look too far because Dave Stone set an example, not only of grace, but of what mission work could look like. "Dave hadn't just dedicated himself to the word of the Lord, but to living in a way that honored Christ's example," explains Carmen.

Carmen's parents, who remained loyal to the Catholic Church, were glad their son wasn't getting into trouble, but his father continued to disapprove of his involvement with the Christian Center and his friendship with Dave.

The rift didn't heal until Babe was 16 years old and Jojo fell terribly ill with a bowel blockage. After Jojo had been on an IV in the hospital for three months, Daisy took him to a specialist in Pittsburgh, who told her there was nothing she could do, and that she should leave him in a sanitarium to die. Daisy wouldn't hear of it. She brought him home, hooked him up to an IV again, and nursed him for several weeks. Then one stormy night, Carmine decided it was time to let Jojo go. He asked Babe to go get the priest, to deliver the last rites. Babe went to the rectory and knocked on the door, but the priest who answered refused to come.

"He told me my family wasn't reputable, that we were destined for hell," Carmen recalls. "We weren't churchgoers who contributed regularly to the church. While my mom prayed the rosary, we didn't fulfill the temporal duties required by the church."

Babe looked the priest squarely in the eye. "Father," he said, "if you get to hell before I do, let them know I'm coming."

He went off in the rain, and near his house he ran into Dave Stone. Babe was crying, and Dave asked him what was wrong.

"All you ministers are alike," Babe told Dave. "Phonies. When we need you, you judge us."

He told Dave what had happened, and Dave offered to come pray with Jojo himself.

"My dad will shoot you," said Babe.

"That's my problem, not yours," Dave replied.

When they got to the house, Babe's parents were confused, but Dave just said, "Mr. and Mrs. Porco, I'm here to pray for your son."

They went into the living room, where there was a bed for Jojo because he couldn't make it up the stairs. Dave stood over Jojo and started to pray. At some point, Daisy told him he needed to go home to his wife, and Dave said, "My wife knows where I am and what I'm doing."

Dave prayed with Jojo all night. In the early morning, he asked Daisy to make Jojo his favorite meal. Daisy looked at him like he was crazy because Jojo had been fed intravenously for some time. Still, at around 8:30 that morning, Daisy went and made him pork and beans with meatballs and brought some in for all of them. Jojo opened his eyes and let Dave feed him.

"By the next day Jojo had color in his face and recognized us," recalls Carmen, still amazed.

From that night on, Babe's dad called Dave "Stony" and leapt to his defense at every chance. Jojo lived 23 more years, dying at 65.

Dave was Babe's lifelong mentor and guiding force. "He was my role model," recalls Carmen. "He walked the walk. He showed me what I could be and how to do for others, even when putting oneself at great expense and risk."

Dave's ultimate lesson in self-sacrifice came about eight years after he arrived in Weirton, when his advocacy for workers' rights and justice started to rub some of the executives from the Weirton Steel Mill the wrong way. The executives, who were on the board of the Christian Center, made it clear to Dave that he needed to stop organizing workers or the mill's funding for the center would be pulled.

"Dave could have stayed quiet, moved on to other things, but he chose instead to do the right thing at a great loss to himself. Dave was fired for his advocacy work. His actions had a huge impact on me," says Carmen.

"I felt so sad for our community to lose a guiding light like Dave" continues Carmen. "I'd assumed when he arrived that he was a spoiled brat from Minnesota, but now I knew that he was so much more—and here he was dealt an unfair hand. It inflamed my anger about businesses that control small towns. I knew then that I was going to study institutions and how they organize and collect power and find ways to challenge them."

After Dave lost his job in Weirton, he went on to a successful ministry in Youngstown, Ohio, and he and Carmen kept in close contact. They visited each other and continued to share ideas about the ministry. Carmen continued to look for something bigger beyond preaching and the walls of one church. He looked back to Reverend Highsmith's ministering to people where they lived and Dave's profound example of mission as a way of living, not just talking. For Dave, the Bible was a way of life, not just the word of God, and through his example he had transformed Carmen. Carmen continued to ask Dave one question: "How can I ever repay what you've done for me?"

Years after graduating from Andover-Newton Theological School, after Carmen started working in communities in Wisconsin, Dave answered the question:

"Look at what you've done in Wisconsin," he told Carmen. "I'm so proud of what you have done with your housing ministry."

CHAPTER EIGHT

Leaving Weirton

CARMEN'S LAST TWO YEARS OF HIGH SCHOOL WENT BY quickly. His teenage years had started out with gangs and trouble, but he now envisioned an entirely new future for himself, moved by his calling to accomplish more than he'd ever dreamed for himself.

He left home in the fall of 1965 for Alderson-Broaddus College, 130 miles away in Philippi, West Virginia. Alderson-Broaddus is a small liberal arts school that was founded by two prominent Baptists in the 1800s. He chose Alderson-Broaddus partly because it was a Baptist school, but mainly because it accepted him despite his mediocre high school grades. He hoped for a fresh start in a place where the exchange of ideas was valued, free questioning was encouraged, and he could come to his own conclusions about the meaning of religion, philosophy, and social justice. The journey out of Weirton found Carmen not only exploring new ideas but beginning to learn that words and ideas weren't enough.

This was the first time Carmen had lived away from home, and he was excited initially; however, his first weeks at college proved to be rocky. Carmen arrived at Alderson-Broaddus amid the frenzy of rush week—when all incoming students were expected to pledge one of the many fraternities or sororities on campus. Carmen knew nothing about fraternities. The Greek system was a strong part of student life at Alderson Broaddus. Rush week brought with it all the typical traditions, good and bad. One would never know, particularly during that week, that the campus was supposed to be dry. To Carmen, the existence of harsh hazing at a Christian school made no sense. He had come to college to expand on his budding theology, to explore new ideas and meet new people, but everyone around him was preoccupied with this tradition that seemed to be concerned mostly with cruel initiations and raucous partying.

"It was a great disappointment," Carmen recalls.

He refused to participate in the Greek system in part because of his Fundamentalist religious beliefs, but he was also looking for more, deeper relationships and connections between the religious and social justice ideas in his head and his own experience. His refusal caused a fair amount of consternation among the fraternities, which expected incoming freshmen to not only participate but to do so with enthusiasm and deference. Those students who didn't participate were ostracized.

Carmen's refusal to join a fraternity or any campus organization created waves at the school. "Fraternities didn't like it, and I got visited by the leaders of some of them," Carmen recalls. "They gave me warnings that I either conform or get out of the college. They said that I didn't belong there. I said, 'No, I don't see it that way. And I'm going to continue to resist you. You just made it more worthwhile.'"

Carmen met with the dean of students to express his consternation with the Greek system. No doubt Carmen's experience behind the pulpit helped him make his case against how the frats were running rush week. The dean was moved by Carmen's arguments, and new rules were put in place for how fraternities could recruit students. Carmen hadn't been on campus but a week, and already he had changed the status quo, which left him with a sense of accomplishment.

Hill Folk

Carmen felt that his ability to speak and generate ideas was all he needed; however, he was coming to see that systemic change required more than just a "silver tongue"—he needed focused action. While he avoided the frats and didn't feel compelled to join any other campus groups, he started his own campus ministry, which was primarily concerned with reaching out to local Appalachians, the *hill folk*, as they were known by most of the students and faculty. Carmen became interested in the hill folk because he felt they were treated like outsiders, just like himself.

This was a risky proposition, however—the hill folk were private and viewed outsiders and town folk with suspicion and contempt. They were extremely independent and self-supporting. Hill folk did not engage with societal institutions and were very distrustful of government. They didn't believe in modern medicine, even though there was a modern hospital right nearby. In fact, Alderson-Broaddus had a national reputation for its nursing program. Carmen worked to bring together the people who lived in the mountains and the services offered by the college.

"They were peaceful except for feuds between families, and they lived close to nature and would come into town just for basic foodstuffs or kerosene, then go back to the hills. Hill folk scared town folk because they were pushy and carried guns," Carmen recalls. "College folk and mountain folk didn't mix—that was the understanding at the time. I didn't understand why, so I decided to go visit the locals and talk to them." Carmen convinced a few of his classmates to tag along.

This was, as Carmen puts it, a stupid move. "We made initial contact by just walking into the woods and knocking on their doors. We figured the woods weren't private property, that anyone could go there, but we were wrong. We violated every rule of conduct you could imagine. We meant no harm, but we were lucky we didn't get shot. They responded by telling us to leave and never come back."

One woman, however, told Carmen he could come back if he came alone. So he did. "When I went back by myself the second time," Carmen says, "one of the leaders who called all the shots sat on a front porch spitting tobacco, and he talked to me. He said, 'We don't want nothing to do with y'uns.' I explained that they had sick kids and there was a hospital right nearby. 'We take care of our own,' he said. 'What makes you think you can help us?'

"I hadn't thought about helping from their perspective. I made all the mistakes from an arrogant, privileged position, thinking only about my side of the equation. But we were allowed to continue visiting that family and others."

Carmen continued to visit and build a rapport with the communities that lived in the mountains. Eventually, more students joined Carmen's outreach, including a nursing student who made inroads with one of the families and was allowed to treat their sick daughter.

"A few days later the girl was well, and this nurse was considered a hero by the hill folk. She became the bridge between the two groups. I had hoped they would bring their kids to the hospital, but that never happened. We always had to go to them," recounts Carmen.

Carmen channeled the verbal skills he had honed as a young preacher, along with his ability to relate to people, to gain entry into the communities of hill folk around Philippi. He was also learning that change involved action. When the chance came to extend his education beyond the classroom and get involved in direct action, he jumped on it.

Milwaukee Mission

One year after starting college at Alderson-Broaddus, in 1966, Carmen was invited by Ray Schroeder, then the executive director of the American Baptists Church Christian Centers, to work as an intern at the Christian Center in Milwaukee, Wisconsin. Specifically, Ray wanted Carmen to intern with the Reverend Ken Smith and work with Father James Groppi, a young Roman Catholic priest who had earned a name among civil rights leaders for his work in leading marches across the city in support of fair housing legislation.

Carmen had known Ken Smith previously, because Smith had moved to Weirton as an American Baptist intern at the Weirton Christian Center prior to Dave Stone's tenure. At the Milwaukee Christian Center, Carmen worked under Smith to promote inclusive housing access and develop youth programs. Carmen studied the methods and messages that Father Groppi employed, but he also began to do the daily work of organizing and activism.

Smith had become a strong advocate of social policy change and a deeply involved member of Father Groppi's activist network. There were few American communities with its neighborhoods as starkly segregated as Milwaukee in the 1960s. For his year in Milwaukee, Carmen lived at the YMCA—now the Marquette Tower—and worked alongside Smith, organizing people and programs through the Christian Center, and videotaping and studying Father Groppi's marches. He was also sent briefly to study "hot spots" in other parts of the country, places where civil rights activity was gaining strength, including Newark and Los Angeles.

Carmen first met Father Groppi at St. Boniface Church, the predominantly African-American Catholic Church he'd led since 1963, during a meeting with other civil rights activists. Carmen began to attend Father Groppi's services and listen to his gripping sermons.

"I was impressed by his command of the intentionality of Jesus," recalls Carmen. "His sermons inspired me to develop my own sermon about that intentionality, which included the five principles of the essence of Christ: unconditional love, nonjudgmental witness, disciplined compassion, the extension of grace, and the covenant of community."

These principles were the keystones of Father Groppi's ministry, and Carmen was moved throughout his year in Milwaukee by the man's deep conviction and integrity. More than his words, though, Father Groppi's example showed Carmen how those ideas could be transformed into action. Father Groppi inspired action, and that action changed Carmen as well.

When Carmen marched with Father Groppi, he captured the experience on film using a Super-8 video camera. On August 28, 1967, Carmen participated in an open housing march alongside Father Groppi from St. Boniface to the 16th Street viaduct—which has since been renamed for Father Groppi. It was known locally as "the longest bridge in the world" because it connected the north side of the city, which was mainly African American, to the south side, which was mainly Polish American.

The marchers were headed for Kosciuszko Park on the south side of the viaduct, in a neighborhood that had welcomed segregationist presidential candidate George Wallace only a few years earlier by singing "Dixie" in Polish. Thousands of white neighborhood residents who had gathered at Crazy Jim's car lot stopped the marchers. The counter protesters threw rocks and bottles, shouted racial slurs, and burned an effigy of Father Groppi. Carmen caught it all on film.

Eventually, Father Groppi's tactics inspired change in Milwaukee's housing laws; however, as much as the priest inspired action across the community, Carmen observed that Father Groppi's white parishioners were less supportive of the priest. While his own congregation was predominantly African American, the bulk of Milwaukee's Catholics were Polish, and they vehemently opposed Father Groppi's marches across the Menomonee Valley viaduct. Eventually the diocese moved and marginalized Father Groppi.

Carmen says, "One of the formative experiences of my year with Father Groppi was seeing how a very religious community can cower out. This was one thing that led me to eventually evaluate the church as a system, too, and consider how churches can be moral cowards. Father Groppi wanted us to think about why we should never oppress any human for any reason. The church often aligns with the oppressor instead of the oppressed, and Milwaukee was no exception."

In addition to studying the marches, Carmen was tasked by Ray Schroeder to work with street gangs on Milwaukee's south side. To reach kids in gangs, Carmen worked with a minister named Gilberto Marrero—known as Reverend G—who started a storefront outreach program called "The Spot." They met with gang members in an old barroom at 6th and National on the south side and developed programs to get kids off the streets and into more productive activities.

Carmen became a dedicated worker, looking for resources and ways to keep the kids from life in the gangs. Here, as in the hills around Philippi, Carmen came to recognize the importance of providing services to people beyond just a religious service: social services, opportunities, and hope. Though it's no longer affiliated with the Milwaukee Christian Center, the United Community Spot, now the United Community Center, remains active on Milwaukee's south side even today and has evolved into an important Latino community institution.

Carmen returned to Alderson-Broaddus following his year in Milwaukee changed, but still focused on his studies. He graduated from

Alderson-Broaddus with a bachelor of science degree in psychology in 1969. He focused his academic studies on how power affected people.

"I wanted to study why people are reluctant to leave their comfort zones and develop a fuller sense of community," Carmen recounts. "I thought psychology would help me to know myself better and also more fully understand traditions and movements. How the form of slavery changes from a plantation to a steel mill, for example, or a football stadium. I learned about the relationships between the powerful and the powerless."

While Carmen received a well-rounded liberal arts education at Alderson-Broadus, the year he spent in Milwaukee revealed to him the kind of ministry he wanted to pursue. He saw that the church could do beneficial work in the community, and he came to believe that pastors had a moral obligation to work to improve people's lives. As he searched for the next step in his life, he looked for a place that would both further his theological learning as well as provide opportunities for social justice work.

Seminary

Carmen rejected the advice of Dave Stone and Ray Schroeder, who had pressured him to choose a Baptist seminary and start a career as a reverend, ministering to a congregation. Instead, he enrolled in Andover-Newton Theological School, located in a suburb of Boston. He had visited the school as an undergraduate, and as he had talked to students and professors there, he had learned that the school not only offered training for the pulpit but was also committed to social justice.

By the time he enrolled in seminary, Carmen had been deeply immersed in the civil rights movement. He read *Stride toward Freedom* and *Letter from a Birmingham Jail,* which helped him better understand

Dr. Martin Luther King Jr. He had watched the speeches of Malcom X and Stokely Carmichael. While these men remained an inspiration to Carmen, by 1969 only one, Stokely Carmichael, was still alive. From their words, and through the example of Father Groppi, Carmen sought to develop a theology of social action.

"People were impressed that I knew so much about direct nonviolent action," recalls Carmen. "I held conversations with theologians and even challenged them. They were so caught up in the power system, they couldn't be prophetic. By then I was starting to question Fundamentalism. I believed it wasn't enough to be saved in your own right—that grace requires us to give, not just receive. I pushed this idea, and I challenged theology that said that our reward was in the Kingdom of God in heaven. I was a firebrand and wanted injustice corrected."

The seminary's emphasis on social justice was supported by the work of three professors who would become important mentors to Carmen: James Luther Adams, Max Stackhouse, and John Belinski. The first and most influential was Dr. Adams, who was a Christian ethicist and studied power and values in voluntary associations. Dr. Adams famously said, "By their group, you will know them." With his experience with gangs, and both resisting and organizing groups of people, Carmen was drawn to Dr. Adams's theology. He and Dr. Adams really clicked, and the friendship they developed would turn out to be one of the highlights of his schooling at Andover-Newton.

Dr. Adams had been part of the Confessing Church, a resistance movement against Hitler's push to unify all of Germany's Protestant churches into a single pro-Nazi Protestant Reich Church.

"I remember going to hear Dr. Adams's lecture at Harvard about Nazi Germany," says Carmen. "He would tell stories about the rigidity of the German mindset, which caused them to follow Hitler's leadership, fatally. He also told of how, before the Gestapo came to find evidence to arrest him for resisting Hitler, Dr. Adams had a carpenter come to put a thin false shelf in all his dressers, and there he hid the resistance papers. So when they ransacked his place, they didn't find the papers. He told that story with such intensity that you felt you were there, watching the Gestapo throw around the furniture and hoping nothing broke. The hairs on your arms would rise as you listened."

After class, Dr. Adams would say, "Carmen, let's go have a light," and they'd go smoke pipes in his office and talk about life, books, and theology. Sometimes they didn't leave until 10 p.m., still smoking Flying Dutchman. Carmen would feel high from the tobacco and their conversation. Dr. Adams talked about the powerful and the powerless. He talked about voluntary association. From his experience in Germany, Dr. Adams had devoted himself to not only a liberal theology but a dedicated activism. In Dr. Adams's work, theology came together with social justice and a focus on group organizing.

Carmen would go on to use Dr. Adams's example in his own housing work years later. His association with and learning from Dr. Adams were where Carmen's mission in housing had its genesis. "'By their group, you shall know them,'" says Carmen, repeating Dr. Adams's famous phrase. "If it isn't just, you have to challenge the system to meet the needs of the minority. You have to promote equality." Reflecting back on that transformational relationship, Carmen recalls, "He took me in and helped me move away from Fundamentalism."

Carmen was also influenced by Max Stackhouse, a professor who studied apartheid in South Africa and argued that the basis of Christian theology was in urban politics and was increasingly relevant to modern social problems. During Carmen's time at Andover-Newton, Prof. Stackhouse was working on his book *Ethics and the Urban Ethos*. In it, he tried to argue for the relevance of Christian ethics in working to solve modern problems related to social justice. However, he was criticized for lacking any clear suggestions for the ways that his proposed groups with a Christian mission may effect change. This was a criticism that Carmen would address through his own example years later. Prof. Stackhouse's arguments provided a path forward for Carmen to imagine his own housing ministry, even if they fell on the deaf ears of academia in 1972.

The third main influence on Carmen at Andover-Newton was Dr. John Belinski, who led the clinical psychology program and was a disciple of Sigmund Freud, Alfred Adler, and Carl Jung.

"I remember Dr. B listening to me talk about why I felt so disadvantaged growing up in a community of poverty. He would say, 'OK, you know this about yourself, so are you going to carry it into your future, or are there steps that you can take to unravel this and make something positive from it?'" Carmen recalls.

Dr. Belinski was hard on Carmen, and he continued to put pressure on him to reimagine his future. "I thought he was crazy," says Carmen, "and it took maybe three months, but he never let up. I could have easily said, 'This guy is mean-spirited and a disciplinarian,' but I learned that wasn't the case. He was a passionate person and took seriously his work of helping people find themselves and remake themselves in a more positive way. I went in there with a chip on my shoulder. I was never an academic or an intellectual—I managed to get Bs in college, but that's about it—but Dr. B helped by telling me I had a unique intelligence and I needed to never lose sight of that. I learned over time that it was true: I do have a unique intelligence born of the barroom and the streets that gave me a deep understanding of human nature and a strong sense of intuition, and I was learning how to use it."

From these three teachers, Carmen not only gained a respect for the power of groups of people to enact change, he was able to reevaluate his own life and gain a new sense of self-respect. He developed a belief in his ability to channel his Christian beliefs into a social mission. Dr. Adams's Christian ethics, Prof. Stackhouse's view towards social change, and Dr. B's relentless faith in Carmen impacted him in many ways, but Carmen was still searching.

Pastor Porco

During his first year at the seminary, Carmen was an intern with the American Baptist Churches of Massachusetts and, at his own request, signed a one-year contract in 1969 as an associate pastor with a church in Holden, Massachusetts, two hours west of Boston. Holden was a wealthy, primarily white community, and it was through this experience that Carmen learned two life-changing truths about his future:

First, he was not cut out to become a traditional pastor, to preach every Sunday to the same congregation; for him, that meant being satisfied with an extremely slow rate of social change. "I loved preaching," Carmen says, "but my usefulness as an agent of change couldn't be put to full effect in that capacity."

Second, he struggled to relate to affluent people. "I didn't know how to small talk the way they did," Carmen explains. He had come from a very direct background, where even though some people had small vocabularies, you always knew what they meant to say.

"I didn't understand them," he says about his congregants in Holden. "That year, I began to form my ideas about the poverty of the wealthy."

To Carmen, the rich congregants of Holden were just as dysfunctional as they supposed poor people to be. One of the broad discourses about poverty is that the poor lack the moral qualities of the rich. Reflecting back on that time, Carmen notes, "I'd assumed that wealthy people were morally superior, but my experience in Holden opened my eyes to that not being so."

The experience also reminded Carmen of his own racial identity. He didn't identify as being white; he was Italian, and Italians had a history of being excluded from white power structures. In that wealthy white congregation, he felt his difference keenly, and he came to embrace it. To this day, he won't sign a form or check a box that labels him *Caucasian*.

"I'll scratch it out and write in 'Italian,'" he says. Carmen believes that the designation of whiteness represents a superior attitude or system of oppression. It was a system that had kept him down in the valley next to the steel mill in Weirton, and even though he had moved on, he still didn't want to move up the same way that some of his relatives had when they made it back home, by buying into the system that kept poor people oppressed.

Carmen didn't visit Weirton while he was in seminary. He lost touch with most of his old friends, some of whom went to Vietnam and didn't come back and some of whom moved away. His parents continued to run the tavern, and when it came time for Carmen to graduate from seminary, his mother stayed behind to keep the business open. To Carmen's surprise, his father came to the commencement ceremony with Carmen's brother Pat.

"At first I wasn't sure what to make of him being there. He'd never expressed approval of my decision, and I wondered if he would lose his temper for some reason and embarrass me," Carmen says. "But he didn't. In fact, he told me he was proud of me and that he loved me. In all my years, he'd never said those words, but he said them that day."

CHAPTER NINE

May Cheyne

FINDING LOVE WAS, FOR CARMEN, A LONG AND WINDING road. In his younger years, he didn't have much luck with girls, and as he grew into adulthood, his luck improved only slightly. With a woman named May Cheyne, however, Carmen found not only love but a partnership that would last for 44 years and help carry him through the many years of his housing ministry.

During his time as an intern in Milwaukee, Carmen had tried to maintain a long-distance relationship with a girl he'd known back in Weirton named Linda. She had been Carmen's first real girlfriend. They'd met through the local Baptist Youth Fellowship. After Carmen left for his Milwaukee internship, he wrote notes to Linda regularly, but eventually he noticed that he wasn't getting any notes from her in return. One weekend, he went back to Weirton for a surprise visit, but the surprise was on him—she was dating other people.

Carmen felt betrayed. "That was my first-ever breakup. After that, I didn't date for a long time," recalls Carmen.

In the summer of 1970, after his third year at Andover-Newton, Carmen and his friend Don Crosby codirected a two-week summer camp for at-risk teenagers and seniors from an inner-city Boston neighborhood. The camp was sponsored by the American Baptist Churches of Massachusetts.

On his first day at the camp, Carmen struck up a friendship with a lifeguard named Evie. The friendship evolved into more, until Carmen learned from another counselor that Evie was engaged to be married within a matter of weeks.

"When I confronted Evie, she told me she was confused. I was devastated and felt deceived. It was unreal, just like it had been with Linda, my first girlfriend," recounts Carmen. Indeed, it was beginning to seem to Carmen that he could not trust women with his feelings.

Carmen turned to another new friend, May Cheyne, a student at Wellesley who had also volunteered for the summer camp, for advice. May advised him to talk to Evie and give her a chance to explain herself by asking her honestly to do so, which he did. Evie explained that she loved her fiancé and that they both wanted to live a farming life. When she'd met Carmen, she had been confused about what she really wanted out of life. Carmen wanted to live in the city and pursue work in social justice, which is what he had told her. They would not have been a good match in the long run.

"I wanted her to be happy," says Carmen, "so I let her go. She was a nice person, and it was unfortunate that we'd started the way we had. I learned to ask more questions before getting too serious about a relationship." His romantic relationships to this point had tested his faith in others, particularly women.

As the summer ended, Carmen headed back to his apartment in Boston's historically Italian north end to finish his studies at Andover-Newton and continue his work with the American Baptist Churches of Massachusetts. Carmen and Don Crosby shared an office, and one day about a month after returning from camp, Carmen walked in the office to find Don on the phone. "You'll never guess who just walked in," Don said into the phone before handing it to Carmen. It was May. As it turned out, she also worked as the babysitter for Don and his wife.

From that point forward, Carmen and May talked on the phone frequently before they made a date to meet at a hamburger joint in Wellesley. Over many burgers and long walks, they found that they shared the same values and aspirations for social change. They talked about philosophy, theology, politics, social justice, and love.

Carmen wasn't always completely comfortable in May's well-heeled world of Wellesley College, but he wanted to impress her. So, after their first date, he decided to take her to a restaurant in Cambridge, not far from Harvard, as a sort of middle ground. When they got off the subway, though, it turned out they were in the wrong place. Carmen couldn't remember exactly where the restaurant was located. They got back on the subway and rode to another stop and got off again. This time, as they climbed the stairs to the street, they were stopped by a homeless man, who asked them for a quarter.

"This guy" recalls Carmen, "you could smell from 10 feet away."

Carmen felt sheepish and caught off guard. He was a minister, and no stranger to poverty, but in his years in Boston he'd learned not to hand out cash on the streets where it would likely go for booze. Still, he was eager to impress May. He paused, trying to decide what to do.

It was May who took charge. "What do you want the quarter for?" she gently asked. The man told May he was hungry. Without missing a beat, May invited the man to join them for dinner.

Carmen wasn't sure how this would play out, but he wasn't going to argue. The man joined them on the short walk to the restaurant. When they approached the maître d', May took charge again by explaining that they had a reservation for two but there was a change in plans and a third would be joining them.

The maître d' looked May and Carmen over, then turned his gaze to the homeless man beside them. Begrudgingly, he took up three menus and started to lead them to a table at the back of the restaurant, right beside the swinging doors to the kitchen.

Again, May spoke up. She politely asked for a table by the window, central to the main dining room.

After they were seated, Carmen could hear grumblings from the other diners about their companion's odor. The man asked for some bread and maybe a sandwich, but May insisted he order off the menu. Carmen was growing anxious. He had no problem with the change of plans, but he did have a pretty serious concern: would he be able to cover the bill, or have to endure the shame of not having enough money? This restaurant was not cheap.

As they ate, May asked the man about his family, his background, and how he'd become homeless. He explained his circumstances, and May nodded in sympathy and asked more questions. Carmen listened, and as he did, he felt he was learning as much about the character of his date as he was about this stranger. She had a grace about her that saw past the surface that so many others used as a base for judgments; she accepted the humanity of this man regardless of how he looked or what others thought. She was confident in doing what was right, even if it made others uncomfortable.

After a while, Carmen recalls, he couldn't even smell the man's odor, and there were no more complaints from other customers. In fact, when Carmen asked, with some trepidation, for the bill, the waiter reported that their meal had been paid for by the woman dining at the next table, who had already left the restaurant.

May had a strong sense of social justice and a surfeit of humanity. "She restored my faith in women," Carmen remembers with a smile.

One day he went out to Wellesley to see May, and as they walked around the campus, he laid it all on the line. He told her, "Look, I can't compete with these Harvard and MIT guys. They have money and I don't, and if you want to go to their mixers, you're free to go. But I have a question for you." Then, he recalls now, he was very forward. He said, "I'd like you to consider marrying me. You don't have to decide right now."

There has long been a legend at Wellesley that if a student walks around Lake Waban three times with the same man passing Tupelo Point, he must propose or be thrown in the lake. Carmen lived up to that legend, and though he didn't get thrown into the lake at that point, May did need time. She had to be sure that Carmen was ready, and that she was ready.

On Thanksgiving that year, Carmen took the train from Boston to May's hometown of Mansfield, Massachusetts, to meet her mother, Ruth Cheyne. May's father had died from a heart attack when she was eight. He had been a naval engineer for Esso and had designed supertankers in Germany and Italy. When Carmen got out of the train station, he started to walk toward town and eventually arrived at the address May had given him, 273 Main Street. Outside, he came upon an unusual scene: the house was surrounded by police with their guns drawn. Carmen backed away and found a pay phone. When May answered, he asked if she was all right, and she said she was. Why was he asking? When he explained, she laughed. "You must be at 273 North Main Street. We live at 273 South Main Street, in a different part of town. Hold tight, we'll come get you," she said.

When they arrived back at May's house, Carmen recalls being overwhelmed right away—not by her mother or sisters or brother, but by the elaborate dining room table, set for a seven-course meal with more utensils and plates and bowls than he could imagine using for one meal.

"Where I grew up," Carmen says, "the pots we used to cook the food in went right on the table, and all we needed was a spoon or a fork."

Without a clue about what utensil to use when, Carmen made careful study of the other dinner guests, including May's sister Debbie and her husband, Harry. Shortly after the meal started, everyone at the table picked up his or her butter knife and shook it. Carmen did as they did, except unlike everyone else's, his butter knife rattled when he shook it. The knives were laid back down on the table, and everyone paused expectantly. May's brother, Jeff, gave him a momentary nasty stare, and Carmen surmised that the young man didn't like him dating his sister. Then dinner proceeded politely.

After dinner, Harry clued Carmen in on the mystery: if your knife rattled, you were supposed to hand it over to Jeff, who was acting as the head of the household since his father had died. It was a family custom. Harry had gotten a kick out of the knife incident. Carmen explained that he hadn't known to hand over the knife because he hadn't been told. It didn't seem to matter much, as conversation become friendlier as the evening wore on. Later, Jeff heard about Carmen's experience with cars and took him for a ride in his Mustang. Carmen remembers it as a wild but fun ride on New England's country roads, thrilling with each twist and turn. They arrived back at the house as buddies.

Thanksgiving was a success. Carmen came out of the experience feeling like he was part of the family. He would often visit Mansfield with May, take trips to her family's beach house, and go sailing with her brother. They were all involved in their local First Baptist church. It seemed that the kindness of May's mother and generosity of spirit had passed down to her children, but May in particular had developed an "honest sense of compassion," notes Carmen. Every time the couple returned for a visit with May's family, Carmen slept in a guest room on the main floor of the large house, among large bookshelves and a fireplace. Indeed, it was a warm home.

They continued to date, spending many lunches together enjoying each other's company and debating over books they were reading. Soon, Carmen asked if she'd given any thought to his proposal. She said she'd thought about it but she didn't yet have an answer. This happened five more times. Each time she would say she didn't have an answer. It is impossible to know what May was thinking at the time. Perhaps she was still making sure that their values and goals were aligned for a long life of partnership, or maybe she was just testing Carmen's faith in her. Finally, after a long afternoon together, she said, "Are you going to ask me again or what?" He said, "No, I'll wait."

"Well," she said, "I have my answer."

His breath caught in his chest as he asked her for the seventh time.

"My answer is that I'd be happy to be engaged to you," she said.

When they became engaged, May was in her last year of college, studying for a major in French and a minor in history and economics, and Carmen was in his last year of graduate school. They had shared stories about their upbringings and families, and Carmen had become a part of her family in Mansfield, but he still hadn't taken her to meet his parents in West Virginia.

They planned a special visit so that he could introduce her. Carmen was perhaps more nervous about May meeting his parents and seeing where he grew up than he had been about meeting her family. Just before they got on the road, they invited Ruth Cheyne to a restaurant, where the plan was that Carmen would ask his future mother-in-law for her daughter's hand in marriage. They enjoyed a lavish meal, but Carmen got cold feet. May gave him meaningful looks to encourage him, but he kept his mouth shut. Finally, at the end of the evening when they were saying their good-byes, Ruth handed over the keys to her car, which they were borrowing to drive to West Virginia to visit his parents, and joked with Carmen, "Well, I hope you'll let me know if you're planning to elope!"

Carmen was mortified. Not only had he failed to make the gesture he'd planned to make, but he also realized that Ruth had known the whole time.

Tongue-tied, he salvaged his dignity by asking Ruth for her daughter's hand. Her response was that she would be glad to welcome him into the family. He thanked her and ducked into the car, sheepish and relieved.

That night on the way to Weirton, hours later than they'd planned to leave, Carmen recalled the last time he'd brought a woman home to meet his parents. His father, who had a knack for brutal honesty, had insulted her to her face. To prepare May for the worst, Carmen reminded her again and again that his father had a tendency to be hurtful and direct. Twenty miles from his childhood home, he started to sweat.

"Don't worry," said May. "I can handle him." Like his father, May also had a penchant for honesty, though of a much less brutal nature.

When they pulled up to the house, Carmen could see his parents through the glass doors, sitting side-by-side on the perch, which was what they called the bar in the tavern. They were waiting. Carmen and May got out of the car, and Daisy came forward to hug them, but his father stayed put. May stepped toward Carmine, who looked about ready to kill someone, and went straight in to give him a hug. Carmen saw his father melt, and in that moment, something changed in his demeanor.

The next morning, Carmen got up to have a word with his early-rising father before the whole house was awake. He recounts:

"He said to me, 'Carmen, I want to go out and pick two flowers, one for your lady and one for Mom.' So he went out and pruned two beautiful roses from his dozens of bushes, and he brought them in and put them in a glass and then asked me if it would be all right if he gave May this flower. So I'm sitting here thinking, I've never seen him give Mom anything; what was this show? Right then, my mother and May came from the kitchen into the bar, and my father, like a little kid, gives one flower to my mother and one to May, saying, 'This is for you.' My mother put hers down on the table, but May took hers behind the bar and set it up with the bottles of booze." Traditionally, only servers went behind the bar. It was considered a signifier of power. "We were all agog because no one went behind the bar; that was the rule. But my father didn't even blink, just said, 'I like that girl.'"

During this first visit, Daisy and May engaged in long conversations in which Daisy talked openly about her difficult childhood and rough history with her man and also shared her observations about the men who came to the bar.

Carmen recalls, after one such conversation, "Then she turns to me and points and says, 'My son's a man, but men aren't no damn good. *Testa di cazzo*—fuck head!' I'd been expecting this kind of nonsense from my dad, but this was my mother." May wasn't bothered, and the two women continued to bond over the next several days of their visit.

Although he was glad the visit had gone so well, Carmen was relieved to drive away with May still by his side. May had met his family, seen the mill and the community he had lived in. She didn't treat it like a spectacle or pity him. She was not uncomfortable in that place; she was just herself the whole time and enjoyed the visit.

Wedding

Carmen and May married on a beautiful summer day in 1971, in the backyard of May's childhood home with about 30 guests in attendance—many ministers they knew from Boston, along with May's college and high school friends. Carmen's parents didn't come—his mom was running the barroom, and his dad had become very sick with his emphysema. His older brother Pat arrived with Dave Stone, and they were both the best men. Don Crosby, who'd been responsible for getting the couple together in the first place, officiated the ceremony.

There wasn't much time for a honeymoon, but the new bride and groom spent two nights in Martha's Vineyard before Carmen was due to report to the maximum security prison at Walpole, Massachusetts, where he was scheduled to do clinical psychology work for a few months as part of his graduate school requirements.

"I jokingly say that I got married and three days later went to prison," Carmen says. "It was a great experience being schooled by the prison chaplain on the ins and outs of cons and being conned, as well as practicing 'reality therapy' with the prisoners, but a sad one at the same time. Even if you could get a prisoner to come around, they had life without parole, and they wouldn't be released."

The seeming hopelessness of the prison was countered with May's graceful optimism at home. May was not only a professional support to Carmen but also a spiritual one.

"I was the one who went to theological school to study the Bible and volunteerism and social psychology," he says, "but May had an intuitive understanding of the Bible, not just verbatim phrases, but the whole interrelated set of stories. As I got older and stopped remembering the stories, a lot of times I'd ask May for help remembering scripture. She was my living Bible."

By this time, Carmen was convinced that he and May shared the same values and passion for social justice. That she was a partner both in love and in faith.

Learning the Ropes

After his graduation, Carmen and May left Massachusetts for New York City, where he began a six-month training program in housing management with the American Baptist National Ministries, which owned low-income housing units all across the country. This training, along with additional work experience, was designed to give individuals like Carmen the skills and knowledge needed to someday become low-income housing managers.

He and May lived on Staten Island, where Carmen helped to manage three towers with 500 units in each. This was Carmen's boots-on-the-ground housing management training.

Before the move, Carmen warned May that the development in New York could be a culture shock compared with her upper-middle-class upbringing in Massachusetts. May was not fazed. May's mother, Ruth, joined them on their initial visit to the development. Before they set foot on the property, Carmen made sure they knew that the appointment would be temporary. He also said that May was free to live at home during that time if she preferred; they could visit each other on the weekends.

"It was like going from the Garden of Eden to the gates of hell," says Carmen. The development was "infested with every kind of social ill—including cockroaches."

They were headed up to the ninth floor of one of the buildings, to see the apartment where they would live while working on-site. The whole place was covered in graffiti and stank of urine. They called the elevator to the lobby, and the doors opened to reveal a man lying on the floor, bleeding. He wore a Good Humor uniform. He'd been robbed and stabbed.

"It was a rough introduction," recalls Carmen.

They called an ambulance. When the Good Humor man had been taken away, they proceeded to the ninth floor and unlocked the apartment door. Inside they were greeted by a line of cockroaches streaming from the ceiling down the walls.

"Think of it this way," said Carmen, trying to lighten the mood, "we go out for groceries, we can whistle for the roaches and they'll carry our bags for us."

Carmen was about to remind May for the third time that she was not obligated to live with him in this place but was interrupted by the sound of gunfire.

"Stay with your mother," Carmen said to May again, but it was his mother-in-law who answered him.

"My daughter married you," said Ruth. "Whither thou goest, she will go."

Later, after they'd left the complex, Carmen asked May what she wanted to do.

"My mother already told you," she said. "I'm here for better or worse. Don't worry about me; just focus on the job."

The assignment on Staten Island lasted less than six months. While he was there, Carmen's primary job was to obtain training in property management. Audrey Woodley, Carmen's supervisor, ruled the place with intimidation and warned Carmen to let the residents know who was in charge. The two did not see eye-to-eye, and Audrey directed the maintenance staff to give Carmen every service call for a clogged toilet. Carmen learned fast how to clear clogs and fix toilets. Audrey might have meant to break his spirit, but instead he gave Carmen a view into the lives of the residents.

"Audrey didn't break my spirit, even if he had a big laugh over it," recalls Carmen. "He taught me how not to be a manager. He was militaristic, and he told me to make residents afraid, to remind them you have the power. But I learned that effective management doesn't use power, it uses conscience."

He learned something else, too: "If you can get a person's toilet working, you're treated like a savior."

May was right there by his side. They were a team.

"Sometimes you think when you marry someone from a certain class and you're working in communities of poverty, it might not be a good fit," says Carmen. "But May always surprised me. She was always there for me and with the people. She had a great feeling for the integrity of poor people." The experience galvanized their faith, both in each other and in their mission to serve poor communities.

From Staten Island, the couple moved to Columbia, Maryland. There Carmen was hired to manage an Interfaith low-income housing project, which was part of the new city. Columbia had been developed in 1967 by urban planner James Rouse with the aid of sociologist Herbert Gans. They believed that communities should be determined by human values, not economics and engineering. High-income, middle-income, and low-income housing were built in the same neighborhood, and all denominations worshipped under one roof. Rouse was adamant that the people who lived at Columbia share the core principles of integration and equality, and everyone was given equal voice in how the community's services were run.

Once, when homeowners were complaining to Rouse about the low-income housing being built right beside their high-income housing, Carmen witnessed Rouse put his money where his mouth was. Rouse said to the homeowners, "Look, I'm going to have my executive secretary meet with you, and you tell me what you want for your house, and I'll buy it from you. We need people here who believe in the concept of a truly integrated community, and obviously you aren't happy here."

"He taught me that there's such a thing as a developer who balances his pocketbook and his conscience," says Carmen.

During that year at Columbia, Carmen had a front row seat to one of the most profound attempts at social change through community building in recent history. One of the most important goals at Columbia was to keep human services on-site, readily accessible to everyone, but, as Carmen witnessed firsthand, this was difficult to implement. What the residents considered "essential" differed by income: swimming pools, in-unit dishwashers, and natural spaces were important to high-income residents, while low-income residents were more concerned about child care, educational opportunities, and job centers.

Columbia was, as Carmen put it, the laboratory where his academic learning from Andover-Newton was turning into reality, and he started to believe in housing as an instrument of change.

"Jim didn't believe in the city form of government. He believed that the Columbia association, a condominium association, was a better vessel for bringing people together. Studying him and working in those communities gave me the understanding that we could do better in housing," Carmen says.

Carmen came to feel that if he could demonstrate institutional change through housing, maybe he could develop a program that would influence the United States Department of Housing and Urban Development (known as HUD), which had been created by President Johnson in 1965.

"These principles of integration gave me a lot of hope," Carmen recalls. This notion of a housing ministry seemed to be the perfect fit for Carmen's life's work. He had discovered how he could use his ministry to directly serve the poor through housing.

After working at Columbia for a year, Carmen was transferred to California to manage the Interfaith housing communities in Riverside, Colton, and Coachella. His mission was to upgrade the management of the properties, including the record keeping and accounting, improve the relationship with residents, and deal with the ongoing challenges of non-community members—namely gang members—who would come into the housing projects and terrorize residents.

"I was a troubleshooter," says Carmen.

All three housing sites included community buildings when they were built, but none were functioning because housing officials wanted them run by an outside agency. Carmen brought residents and outside agencies together to begin taking ownership of the community buildings and offer services, like Head Start.

Riverside was the most problematic site in Carmen's jurisdiction. The manager before Carmen had been murdered, and it wasn't unusual to hear gunshots close by. May and Carmen had even taken refuge once in their tub as gunfire tore through their apartment, leaving a slug in the wall. Part of the problem, in Carmen's estimation, was the friction between African-American and Latino gangs over territory.

Carmen took action after an avoidable tragedy: a man died of a heart attack because the family had been involved in gang activity and the authorities weren't called in time. Carmen called a meeting with leaders of two main gangs and asked for help keeping gang activity off the property. He remembered Bobo Young's plea to use his gifts to get kids off the street and the lessons from Dave Stone, who had faith in his ability to be a force for good.

Carmen spoke to the gang members as brothers and asked them to take on the responsibility of helping keep residents safe. He told them that only with their help could he open a day care center and start educational programs, but none of it could happen without their commitment. Carmen believed that even if the gangs weren't interested in these programs themselves, that they would want them for their parents and brothers and sisters.

"I was so nervous when I left that meeting that I was shaking," he recalls. "But it worked. The people understood that I believed in them at the highest level, and the violence stopped."

A month or so later, a police officer drove up to Carmen's office and asked him what was going on—they hadn't had a call to Riverside in weeks. Such was the result of Carmen's pulling together of all the lessons he had learned from his time on the streets from Weirton to Milwaukee, along with the theology he had developed speaking at Baptist churches across West Virginia, into a management style that was proving very effective. He and May were now ready to face even bigger challenges.

CHAPTER TEN

Scum Lord

AFTER PROVING HIMSELF IN NEW YORK AND MARYLAND and getting housing properties in Coachella, Riverside, and Colton, California, operating smoothly—while drastically reducing violence on the properties—Carmen was full of ideas for developing transformational housing management programs. He would soon get the chance to put those ideas in action, as the American Baptist Housing Ministries called him to a new job as a low-income housing manager in Madison, Wisconsin. Carmen had visited Madison a few times during the 1960s and had thought it was a beautiful, small city. He and May accepted the offer.

"Working with low-income housing in New York, Maryland, and California gave me the opportunity to look at how government housing programs could be an avenue for enhancing people's decision-making and improving their own lives. By the time I got to Madison, I'd figured out a lot of pieces of the puzzle. It was about power structures and not personalities," says Carmen. In Madison, he had the chance to lead by confronting the power structures that had defined low-income housing in Madison, but first he had to deal with a few personalities.

The American Baptist Housing Ministries owned buildings in both Madison and Milwaukee. Of the two locations, Madison would prove to be Carmen's greatest challenge. Packer and Northport are two separate properties that are directly across the street from one another in Madison. From Carmen's perspective, Packer and Northport Apartments were disasters. He arrived in the midst of a rent strike with a class action suit brewing. The two housing sites were notorious in the area for their highly mobile resident populations, stuck in a cycle of poverty that the landlords did more to propagate than to mitigate. Both complexes were close to 50 percent vacant, and both mortgages were in default. The properties also had a reputation for crime and prostitution.

The management culture, as Carmen saw as soon as he visited the property, was belligerent and placed little trust in the residents themselves. This was exactly the kind of leadership Carmen had seen fail in his earlier positions. He had no intention of allowing the status quo to continue under his watch, but the people in Madison who were working to limit the power of the city's so-called "scum lords"—landlords profiting blindly off low-income residents with little or no other housing choices—didn't yet realize that they had an ally in Carmen. Nor did they have any trust that he would be different than his predecessors.

Carmen knew that drastic change was needed, but he also understood it wasn't that easy to make change. The complexes were operating under a labor-union type of agreement drafted by the Packer and Northport Tenant Organization (PANTO), which was supported by the liberal power base in the city. A number of the mayor's staff and other advocacy groups in Madison had established PANTO. It was modeled on Saul Alinsky's community-organizing tactics for creating meaningful community change. Alinsky posited that change comes from working mostly within the system and that power comes from two sources: money and people. So those without money must rely on "flesh and blood" to gain power, and change agents must never decrease pressure, but force the opposing faction to live up to its own promises.

"While this was inherently good, there was no model or infrastructure that allowed poor people to represent and lead themselves. These well-intentioned activists were making decisions for people without any firsthand experience of being tenants subjugated to landlords in the court system," says Carmen. They were, just like the previous managers at Northport and Packer, operating on the assumption that they knew better than the residents what they needed.

So what was Carmen's first move as property manager in Madison?

"My time with Father Groppi had taught me that in order to make change happen, you needed tree shakers and jelly makers. I could almost hear him say, 'Shake that tree!' So I tore up the labor-union agreement. It was one-sided. Of course, when I did that, the conflict really started."

Carmen didn't disagree with PANTO's mission or its strategies, even when they worked against him, but he was reluctant to commit to an agreement that perpetuated an assumed antagonism between the management and residents. Fundamentally, that would not work with Carmen's vision for building a system based on a mutual relationship. It also didn't help that by inheriting Packer and Northport, he'd also inherited the reputation of the former landlords—which made him *The Scum Lord* in PANTO's estimation.

As a result, Carmen went toe-to-toe with Madison's liberal power establishment.

"Most of those individuals were good people," Carmen says. "They cared sincerely for other people. But it wasn't enough to care about poor people. At the time, it seemed to me that they were unable to envision and trust that low-income people could voice their own concerns and come to effective, collective resolutions."

While Carmen didn't agree with their tactics, and it was clear that what they were doing wasn't working, he had to develop working relationships with the powers that be in Madison at the time. One of those people opposing "scum lords" was Mayor Paul Soglin.

When Carmen moved to Madison, Paul Soglin had been in office one year of what would turn out to be the first of three separate stints in office. Like Carmen, Soglin had been active in the civil rights movement in the 1960s, including working to convince real estate agents to show and sell suburban homes to African Americans. In the late 1960s, Soglin made a name for himself as a war protestor, in particular during the University of Wisconsin-Madison demonstrations against Dow Chemical Company's campus presence. When Soglin became mayor the first time after serving as an alderman, much of the protest energy had turned away from war to the arena of low-income housing. "There had been a shift from organizing around war protests in Madison toward low-income housing and a strong feeling among liberals that they needed to protect poor people's interests," says Carmen.

Never one to start slow, Carmen set up a meeting with the mayor after only two weeks on the job. His primary goal was to rally the mayor's support for pressuring Wisconsin's Sen. William "Bill" Proxmire to get Section 8 funds released so the true cost of the housing rentals weren't borne directly by the residents, who couldn't pay. As soon as the meeting was underway, Carmen discovered that the mayor was not inclined to support any Packer and Northport owner under any circumstances. He positioned himself squarely against Carmen as the manager, and just when Carmen didn't think the meeting could get any worse, the mayor called him a *scum lord* to his face. "The biggest scum lord in town," said the mayor.

When he reflects on that first failed face-to-face meeting with the mayor, Carmen still wrestles with the conflicting feelings he experienced at the time—confusion, anger, and humiliation, mixed with a glimmer of understanding of the mayor's perspective, and even a begrudging respect for the intensity of the other man's commitment, which, unknown to the mayor, mirrored Carmen's own intense commitment.

"My predecessors had been atrocious," says Carmen. "The mayor was passionate about bringing an end to the oppression of low-income people, and he assumed I was one of the oppressors. That first meeting didn't get very far."

Maybe a different person with a different background would have calmly explained the changes and improvements he intended to make to the properties, or painted a picture of the communities he hoped to build with the mayor's assistance, but Carmen wasn't prepared to defend his years of work with the poor, to have his hard-earned record summarily dismissed—and he was extremely unprepared to be called names.

Carmen's first instinct was to fight, but not with his fists. Carmen was determined to teach Mayor Soglin a lesson. At home, his wife May counseled patience and understanding. Carmen set out to show the mayor that they were on the same side, but he felt he needed to do it in a way that would leave a lasting impression.

His next step was a bold one. Pulling from his days filming the Groppi marches and protests in Milwaukee, he once again took up his video camera. This time, however, he knocked on the doors at the public housing sites run by the city of Madison and asked residents to tell him on camera what it was like to live in the city's housing complexes. Their homes were technically managed by the mayor's office, after all.

The picture painted by the interviews was not pretty. With plenty of footage in hand, Carmen called Mayor Soglin and asked again for a meeting. To his credit, the mayor set one up right away and brought several department heads into the room with him. The atmosphere went sour, however, as soon as Carmen's footage started to roll. Only a few minutes in, the mayor shut off the video and launched into a tirade

Charles Taylor

against his own housing staff, laying the poor conditions of the city housing on their shoulders.

Carmen intervened. He hadn't come to get people fired; he'd come to show the mayor that he was serious about improving his communities, and he was willing to start by asking the residents themselves to speak up in their own voices. City housing and community housing faced similar challenges, and it was time to work together to find solutions.

"It became evident that he understood that maybe I was the biggest scum lord on the private side, but he was the biggest one on the public side," says Carmen. "We had a lot in common, and we were facing the same obstacles and the same steep battle toward progress that neutralized our power imbalance. We were finally off on the right foot."

Now with the mayor on his side, Carmen could shift his focus to getting the Section 8 funds released that he needed to improve conditions at the property.

At this time, President Nixon had impounded Section 8, a federal housing assistance program that provides rental assistance for low-income families. Section 8 is a program where the government provides a subsidy to landlords for the difference between what a resident can afford to pay based on their income and the determined market rental rate of a unit. With the subsidy payments impounded, the residents were expected to pay the market rate for their housing regardless of their income, which for many wasn't affordable and often resulted in large amounts of debt. This made for tough choices between paying rent and buying food, clothes, or other vital things; missed rent payments would result in eviction and tremendous difficulty finding future housing.

Subsequently, the properties didn't have the money they needed to continue operation, let alone transform themselves into communities of opportunity. Carmen knew if he could get the Section 8 funds released, he could not only provide relief for the residents but also eliminate the hated title "scum lord" once and for all. So he went to Washington, D.C., to meet with Senator Proxmire. Going in, Carmen knew it would be an uphill battle—he'd been warned that Proxmire had voted against Section 8 assistance. So why would he now reverse course and work to get the funds released?

This would be a real test of Carmen's powers of persuasion.

Proxmire's secretary arranged for Carmen to have a few minutes of the senator's time. The meeting started cordially, and Carmen explained the basic problem. There were 3,700 residents under his management who could be assisted by the Section 8 funds, but the funds had been impounded and he needed the senator's help to get them released.

"You do realize," the senator said to Carmen, "that I voted against those appropriations?"

After that, Carmen says, "I know my mouth started moving, but I don't know what came out of it."

When Carmen was finished talking, the senator called in his secretary and asked him to write a letter to open hearings on the Section 8 impoundments. He asked the secretary to give Carmen a copy and let him add anything he wanted to add. Then he told Carmen to have a good day and returned to the senate floor.

Carmen was astonished. He had no idea what he'd said. He asked the senator's secretary to fill him in, and the secretary said he'd never heard anyone speak to the senator the way Carmen had. He told Carmen that he'd said to the senator, "Sir, you have every responsibility to do what is right in your conscience for your constituents. But after something becomes a matter of law, you have the same responsibility to get the full benefit of the laws to your people—and, senator, I believe we're in the latter case."

Back in the senator's office, the secretary typed up the letter the senator had requested and gave it to Carmen to look over.

99

Carmine, Pat, Jojo and Daisy Porco

Babe at two
years old

Brother Pat's wedding reception

Babe at eight years old

Carmine in front of tavern construction

The old Wine Press
Carmine used to make
"Dago Red" wine

Miss Daisy waving in doorway of Porco's Tavern

Babe at 14;

Babe in Porco's bar

Babe at 18,
Young Pastor

Dave Stone with kids at Weirton Christian Center

Carmen and May's wedding day

*Carmen breaking ground for
Community Learning Centers in Milwaukee WI*

Standing: Carmen and John: Sitting Dorothy, May and Margaret

Carmen and May at the Lake House prior to her death

Anthony "Cheech" Porco, George Fleming and Carmen

Carmen, Kathy and Buddy

Kathy Martinson-Porco

Greentree Low Income Housing Complex in Milwaukee

Wedding of Carmen and Kathy with Rev. Archie Ivy

"I couldn't think of a thing to add; I just wanted to get out of there" remembers Carmen. "I felt like I'd just robbed a bank and needed a clean getaway. I'm sure that my remarks hit a nerve about the plight that many low-income people were experiencing nationwide."

About six weeks later, Carmen was given the news: his properties in Madison were getting Section 8 subsidies. As a result, the rent strike was settled, the class action suit never materialized, and Carmen was never called a *scum lord* again.

When Carmen was able to announce that all of the residents would pay according to ability, public opinion in Madison's liberal community shifted. His relationship with the mayor improved dramatically as well.

The property management job that he had inherited had long been considered an enemy of the poor; now Carmen had wiped the slate clean.

"It was a blessing that I found Madison when I did, in the midst of a rent strike and with a class action suit brewing," Carmen says. "I anchored here and went after what I believed was right. When I was able to get the Section 8 funds dispersed, the people knew that my philosophy of management wasn't vindictive. I promised the people that I would treat them with dignity, and that's what happened."

Carmen knew that stabilizing the rent situation was only part of the solution. The properties still had debts outstanding from prior to his arrival. Carmen worked with the accountant, named Ken Dobberfuhl, to manage what little money they had to pay back vendors and lenders. They also worked together to imagine a future of financial viability and strength. While Carmen provided the vision and passion, Ken built an accounting system that helped bring that vision to reality. Carmen needed a way to bring services directly to the tenants and find a way to pay for them. From the beginning of his tenure in Wisconsin, he'd been engaged in an ongoing battle with the state of Wisconsin over paying property taxes, which he had made clear that he paid under protest.

"I couldn't understand why some organizations were exempt and low-income family housing with nonprofit status wasn't," Carmen emphasizes. "Country clubs, fraternities and sororities, and so on— they were all exempt from paying property taxes, so why weren't we?"

Carmen went straight to the source that laid out who paid property taxes and who didn't, the city assessor's handbook. In Carmen's study of the handbook, he determined that it wasn't clearly defined which groups were determined to be a charity and which weren't.

"We were Section 8, we were low-income family housing, and we deserved exempt status," he says. "I wanted to make it happen without a big legal battle, which could stall the process for years."

After six years of lobbying key politicians and allies, Carmen was able to earn exempt status for his developments by getting officials to include more specific language in the city assessor's handbook. Carmen suddenly had *extra* funds in his budget. This was a huge accomplishment and meant that he now had the funds to create a model for his housing ministry that he hoped would help lift residents out of poverty.

Carmen's ability to navigate the many personalities and power relationships across the political and social spectrum had created change, but it did not happen overnight. The sort of institutional change that Carmen spearheaded required all of his passion, energy, and life experiences. It had been a long battle, but the political and economic framework were almost in place for Carmen to build the type of community he had been envisioning with May.

Despite his victory in getting his housing units exempt from paying property taxes, Carmen has had to remain forever vigilant since then to maintain the tax-exempt status of his properties.

"About 10 years after we received the exemption, we were asked to prove that we were still performing an exempt service. Every two years, we have to prove that we are serving very low-income people," Carmen explains. "Also there's a 10-acre limit per housing unit, so anything over that is taxable. At our Greentree property in Milwaukee, we're at almost 14 acres, so the units outside of the 10 acres are taxed."

With a lower cost structure all set due to lower property taxes, the next step was to convince HUD not to decrease its subsidies, and to allow those "extra" funds to go toward on-site social services and community learning centers. Locally, HUD officials agreed, but offering on-site social services went against the national thinking of the time, which was that housing is about providing shelter and shelter only.

"Our philosophy was the opposite," says Carmen. "When outside nonprofits come in to dictate to the people, rather than collaborate with them, the chain of oppression continues. Instead, we wanted to provide jobs and services within our low-income housing community, to give members control over their own institution, its resources, its management, its problems, and its solutions."

This way of promoting community through housing wasn't only better for the residents, Carmen argued, it was more cost-effective and efficient for society.

"This is one reason we haven't made a dent in poverty nationally," says Carmen. "Initially when President Lyndon Johnson started his war on poverty, I thought, 'Great, the government's really going to help people,' but then as I watched it progress, I realized it was a farce." Because employment and educational services were not combined with housing, poverty as a system continued and, in many ways, was further ingrained. All the departments and social services Johnson had inaugurated in his war on poverty ended up doing less for the poor than for the white middle class by providing jobs for a new educated class that resulted from the GI Bill at the end of World War II.

There weren't many African Americans who received the GI benefit. The African Americans came up north, ran the industrial machinery, then the war ended and they were displaced in jobs and housing. They weren't allowed access to education. The GI Bill created higher education opportunities primarily for whites. Then came the War on Poverty that situated these whites as helpers for the people of color who had been systematically oppressed by segregation and racism.

Ultimately Carmen was not just trying to shed the title *scum lord* but was also trying to change the system that rewarded scum lords. Madison would have to realize that the system was *scum* and that the people who had navigated that system successfully were, as they had been for thousands of years, *lords*. Carmen and May were very much swimming upstream to try to undo the power structures that had been built by this system. In spite of Carmen's recent success, and in some ways because of it, their life would be turned upside down before they could take the next step in developing the housing that Carmen was working towards.

Carmen discovered that the American Baptist Housing Ministries kept what was known as a "pool fund," which was meant to help siphon money from stronger housing projects to help weaker ones. Now that his properties were making money, the head of American Baptist Housing Ministries, as it was called at the time, and the treasurer requested that Carmen transfer funds from the properties that he managed into the pool fund so they could use the monies for a different project, much like the private, for-profit companies were doing. Carmen refused.

"I asked them to request it in writing from HUD, but otherwise I didn't believe that was the intent of the funds in its original contract, let alone certainly not within the parameters that HUD would have approved. So I refused, and they were angry. The treasurer left, and I didn't hear any more about it, until several months later when I was on vacation."

When Carmen returned from vacation, he was fired.

CHAPTER ELEVEN

Support Community

CARMEN AND MAY WERE BEGINNING TO SETTLE INTO Madison after their many moves. May had enrolled in graduate school, and they were starting a family. All of a sudden, Carmen was without a job. Fortunately, Carmen and May had done more than lay down roots; they had built a support community in Madison. They had developed friendships, and they had faith in the people around them.

Carmen, in particular, had parlayed his early success with Madison's political establishment to build up social and political capital. He had even been elected as the treasurer of the state Democratic Party. He had also developed a reputation with HUD for his ability to turn properties around. All of this political capital would come in handy. Ironically, Carmen's termination turned into an incredible opportunity: not only to continue managing the six properties in Madison and Milwaukee that the American Baptists owned, but to become a property owner himself and create an organization with the values and mission that represented the institutional change he hoped to proliferate. It was the support community that he had built at the properties that not only carried him through this challenging time but would also carry his vision into a successful reality over the next 20 years.

When he was fired, Carmen found his staff upset and ready to protest his firing. While Carmen was caught off guard to learn what had transpired, he didn't want upheaval and unrest, and he also didn't want his staff to risk their job security.

"I asked the staff not to get involved in the issue of my termination because I would deal with it myself, but I told them that if they wanted to be helpful, they should continue fulfilling the mission of our work," Carmen recalls. "I asked them not to get caught up in the politics, because in any situation, I said, each party is half responsible and at fault, and that included me and I would handle my half but make sure that the others handled the other half. I would get it resolved."

That same week, a board member named Fairbanks Cooper learned about Carmen's termination and called HUD to see if that organization had been made aware of the change. They hadn't. Word of Carmen's summary dismissal got back to the regional director of HUD, and he called Carmen and asked him to call him at home, any hour, day or night. Fortunately, Carmen had a very positive working relationship with HUD. They respected the work he had done to turn the properties in Madison around, and he had earned credibility with the agency. When Carmen got in touch with the regional director of HUD, the man firmly stated, "We've had it with the American Baptists. We want to move ahead in a different direction." They wanted Carmen to take over the six properties in Madison and Milwaukee from the American Baptists. HUD also needed someone to take over a property on the south side of Madison and provide adequate housing for the residents. When they discovered that Carmen was now available, they approached him quickly. Carmen recounts the ensuing series of events:

"The HUD administrator said to me, 'Go look at Bram Hill Apartments on the south side of Madison—we want you to take it over as the owner.' I went and looked early Monday morning and agreed to consider it. I needed about $250,000 in grant money to fix up the 34 townhouses. I met with HUD and an attorney that afternoon. They had the paperwork and told me to come by Friday, and they would transfer the ownership to me. 'Are you willing to assume the mortgage?' they said. I said—, 'Are you willing to allow me to raise the rent over the short term to make sure that all of my expenses can be covered?'"

Carmen agreed to assume the mortgage on the condition that he got the grant money for improvements, continued to receive the Section 8 subsidy, and be allowed to raise the rent $200 per month.

"I didn't have a dollar to complete the transaction, so I turned to the HUD attorney and asked to borrow a dollar," he smiles.

Before parting ways, the HUD attorney asked Carmen how much due diligence he'd done and if he'd looked at the Bram Hill community police records.

"If I had," replied Carmen, "I wouldn't be here."

HUD also wanted Carmen to assume responsibility for all six of the American Baptists projects in Wisconsin if they severed the contract, but Carmen declined. He felt it might lead to a lawsuit if he acquired management of the properties that way and wanted the people who had fired him to be held accountable for their misdeeds, which wouldn't happen if they were removed wholesale from the project.

Instead, Carmen was invited to a meeting with the American Baptists official who had ordered him fired, as well as the local board of directors, which included Fairbanks Cooper. But when the man who had fired Carmen learned that Carmen would be in the meeting, he refused to attend and sent a messenger instead. He said he'd talk to the board but not if Carmen were present. The board decided this was unacceptable, and Fairbanks Cooper, along with the rest of the board, supported a resolution to terminate the National Housing Ministries' contract with the six properties and rehire Carmen on their own. This allowed Carmen to take responsibility for the properties without HUD's intervention.

He was now free to continue to develop and implement a housing model, but now he could do it on his own terms, guided by his own experiences and vision. For Carmen, this meant starting by respecting the dignity of people in poverty and trusting them to manage their own communities. He had to build that dignity and trust into the systems and documents at the core of the day-to-day operations of the properties.

The binary resident-management relationship was evident to Carmen in every document, policy, and practice used in his Madison and Milwaukee properties, including leases, which gave owners the right to evict while the residents had little recourse or opportunity to improve their lot or to make changes to address issues. If Carmen were going to succeed in throwing out this binary way of thinking, he'd have to examine every document, every process and procedure, every employment opportunity, and every training and orientation program offered by his housing communities. First, however, he had to hire a staff that understood how to bridge the chasm between resident and manager. To Carmen, the solution was obvious—hire residents.

Years earlier, before Carmen understood the potential of communities like Packer and Northport, a big developer told him not to expect much from the residents of his low-income houses. Carmen asked why not and was told that in such communities there wasn't the kind of leadership available that Carmen would need to realize his goals. Carmen knew from his own experience and background in Weirton that the developer was wrong.

Carmen knew the potential for leadership was in the properties; he just needed to identify it. He observed the residents in the communities, looking for those that had a quiet guidance and natural presence of leadership in the community. He hired on-site resident managers that reflected these qualities. When he went to build his community learning centers on-site and develop a program focus, he again looked for residents to hire.

Identifying Leaders

Before building his learning centers, Carmen started putting out feelers among residents, collecting information he could get only from people who lived in the communities full-time. If they had to pick a leader for themselves, who would they pick? The same names came up over and over. Among his Packer, Northport, Greentree, and Teutonia properties that he managed in Madison and Milwaukee, he collected the names of about eight people who stood out to their peers as potential leaders.

Carmen kept his eye on these eight people to see what their daily routines looked like. He found that the people who had earned respect in their communities were already deeply invested in helping their neighbors and strengthening their communities—they just weren't officially being paid for it yet.

The first residents Carmen approached about becoming program coordinators were Pathoomal (Pat) Wongkit at Northport and Jacki Thomas at Packer. Both women had displayed the values and people skills that Carmen needed to build a successful housing ministry, but it took time and convincing before they accepted the jobs. Jackie had been born into a farming family and was the oldest of six children. She and her husband, Dave, and their three children had been homeless before becoming Packer residents in 1984. In the summers, Jacki was already running work programs for the residents—she'd be doing the same thing on a greater scale in the new position. She had no experience with computers, she told Carmen, and she wasn't sure she could learn.

Pat Wongkit had come to the United States from Thailand during the Vietnam War. Her English wasn't perfect, and she had children she was working multiple jobs to support. When Carmen started painting a picture for Pat of the community he was hoping to build, with learning centers on-site that would house all kinds of educational and job opportunities for residents and a computer lab, Pat looked at him like he was crazy. "Why me?" she asked Carmen. He invited her to be in charge of the technology and educational programs. In a soft voice, she told him she couldn't do it. Carmen persisted. He believed she already assumed what he would call a leadership role in the community, helping neighbors in all kinds of ways. But it wasn't the leadership that worried Pat, it was her language skills.

"Pat," Carmen told her, "you have an innate ability to understand people and bring out the best in them. You treat everyone with respect. I can get you language and computer training, but I can't teach values. You already have those."

Pat was interested, but she was worried that she would be unemployed in three months if she wasn't a good fit. Carmen told her he didn't operate that way. "It's going to take two years to fill this role," he said. "In those two years, learn as much as you can about the people and vision and philosophy of our organization, and the rest will come naturally."

Jacki was still mulling Carmen's offer, worried that she wouldn't be able to do all the things that might be required of her. Carmen talked to both women about supporting each other. His management style was about learning together. All he would do was ask them to do their best. As long as they were honest with each other, he would support them through the learning process.

Pat and Jacki were two different personalities, but each had a similar devotion to their communities. Together, the two women, working across the street from each other, developed a number of powerful educational and community development programs over the next 30 years.

While Pat radiated a quiet and persuasive positivity, Jacki was extremely passionate about changing the system of poverty that had oppressed her. She didn't always see eye-to-eye with Carmen, but there was no denying her success. Over more than two decades, the three of them not only exchanged ideas and philosophies about how to improve the lives of people in poverty—often in heated debate—but they implemented many programs that helped the community develop a sense of itself, as well as a sense of hope.

In Carmen's mind, one can't provide hope to people who are hopeless—one can provide support, but people have to find their own hope. Jacki was relentless in her work to provide hope, no matter what obstacle was in her way.

For Jacki, one of the essential elements in building hope within a community was providing opportunities for creative expression. In her role as a program coordinator, she found ways for the Packer kids to express themselves through a variety of different mediums. Together with the kids, she made films that functioned as living documents of the integrity and humanity of the Packer and Northport communities. She and the kids came up with plots and storylines and once even got the governor's wife, Jessica Doyle, to play a role—Eleanor Roosevelt—in a full-length feature.

One of the things that made Jacki so successful was that she was always pushing for more. At one point, Jacki worked with a group of kids to develop and present a proposal for a recording studio on-site. Carmen had seen what they could do, and he approved the proposal with an addendum that they would get an increased equipment budget. "One of the traps that people without hope can fall into is the belief that they don't deserve something better," Carmen points out. Carmen, along with Jackie's constant pressure, made sure to provide the resources that reinforced the belief that the residents deserved whatever they could imagine. The young people managed the studio for five years.

They cut records, produced songs, recorded poetry slams, and made and edited films in the studio. Five young people had initially come to Carmen with their proposal; in the end, the studio supported programs for more than 60 young people.

On the other side of the street, Pat was also working tirelessly. Pat and her husband had a baby girl shortly after she started as a program coordinator. She had her hands full, but due to the trust that was implicit in Carmen's management model, Pat was often able to bring the baby to work with her. She regularly worked with all the Northport children and their various schools and teachers to build and strengthen relationships between the students, their families, and the schools. Pat would find out what each student struggled with in order to support and encourage that student's development in education during his or her time at the community learning center. She similarly expanded her own potential, developing not only her language skills but also her technological expertise, ultimately earning a degree in computer networking.

Eventually, knowing she wanted to be able to speak to groups the way Carmen did, Pat signed up for a Dale Carnegie public speaking course. She improved her speaking, gaining some confidence, and then one day Carmen put her to the test. He told her he was double-booked to speak in two places at once and asked her to take his place at an event at Edgewood College in Madison. At first, Pat declined. She wasn't ready, she said, but Carmen pushed her.

"You don't have to be me," he told her. "You do it your way."

Carmen sneaked into the back of the venue while Pat was speaking, and during the Q&A after she spoke, she spotted him in the audience. "You got me," she admitted when they had a chance to talk afterwards. "Now I think I'm as good as you are-—maybe better!"

In Milwaukee, Carmen was also on the lookout for a program coordinator. He was determined to hire a resident, someone who was as invested in improving the lives of the members of the developments as he was, like Pat and Jackie.

At the top of the list of candidates was Vicki Davidson, who had come to Greentree as a divorced mother on welfare but had a reputation for her optimistic spirit and drive. No matter what difficulties life delivered, Vicki never seemed to complain.

"Vicki did not have an easy life," says Carmen. "She was raising a son on her own and also taking care of her brother and her mother. She'd been abandoned by her husband, got her college degree in Milwaukee at Alverno College, and was on her way to developing a career. Other residents told me that she didn't complain, that she dealt head-on with hard things and didn't call attention to herself, and that she helped residents even though she could use a hand herself from time to time—and she was a person of faith."

Like Jacki and Pat, Vicki was reluctant to accept the position when Carmen first made the offer. Like her two colleagues, she wasn't confident she could do the job. Carmen knew, however, from observing Vicki and talking to her, that she was deeply committed to helping her neighbors and could parlay that commitment into an official capacity.

When Vicki finally agreed to fill the program coordinator position, she took to the role right away. She earned respect in the community by setting high expectations for people, which nurtured an environment in which people felt encouraged to overcome their own obstacles. She became known as Miss Vicki, which says something about the community's respect for her.

Carmen was impressed with Vicki's contribution to the ministry from the start.

"She really knew how to listen carefully to people's needs and not get sucked into doing for them what they could do for themselves. I've seen her now through the deaths of her close friends and her brother, as well as in anguish about her mother's level of care needs, and she always attempts to be positive for other people. She's helped numerous kids get into higher education and more young adults get their acts together, and she has found ways to create a program that always celebrates their achievements and their destiny. She's a joy to work with, and she gets so much pleasure from the success of others."

Not only did Vicki make clear her expectation of hard work and success from the residents at Greentree and Teutonia, she set the example: she went on to earn a master's degree while continuing to work at Greentree. Her son eventually left for college in St. Louis and became an engineer. She's been on the job for 21 years.

Like Jacki Thomas and Pat Wongkit in Madison, Vicki Davidson has been instrumental in not only encouraging dozens of young people to go to college—to break the cycle of poverty—but also in providing the programs, resources, and hope they needed to get there. Their example is stunning in a housing system that at times is more bent towards oppression than justice. These women have been loyally and diligently working in these communities with Carmen for a combined 60 years.

What is more impressive is that, in an industry with a high degree of turnover—where Carmen himself spent his early career bouncing around the country from job assignment to job assignment—many of his property managers on-site have been with him for even longer than the program coordinators. Like the program coordinators, their lives also reflect the power of Carmen's housing model to empower people.

Jean Knuth, the property manager at Greentree Apartments in Milwaukee, grew up in the community. She started working with Carmen before she had finished high school and has worked at the Greentree community for over 40 years. "Jean is one of the most dedicated, organized, and professional managers that you will ever find," attests Carmen. She not only built an impressive professional life at Greentree, she is emblematic of how integrated housing services can benefit the whole family. Jean, now married and a grandmother, began as an on-site manager but eventually bought a home, though she continues to be an integral part of the fabric of the Greentree community.

"She knows the management system, the regulations, and the processes to the point where she may be able to do much of her job in her sleep," Carmen avers. "Her expertise and example are a testament to what can happen when patience, compassion, and respect form the foundation of property management." Jean is not the only example of residents taking on managerial roles and growing the community and their families over time beyond the confines of the communities within which they work.

Sandra Willis-Smith is the property manager at Packer Apartments in Madison. She came to Madison from Illinois in order to give her kids a safer life with greater opportunity. She has worked with Carmen for 39 years. Sandra has a care and compassion for other residents and, like the others, goes above and beyond to serve them and fold them into the community and all it has to offer. She raised three boys, all at Packer, who have all been, or continue to be, leaders within that community. One of her sons has completed college and moved on to work in nonprofit management in another state. Sandra has trained other office staff in the philosophy and management model, as well as helped manage other properties or assist in the training of new property managers. She is a prime example of how this good work is spreading organically beyond the footprint of the six properties that Carmen has managed.

Carmen's longtime assistant director, Keith Atchley, has been with him for 40 years. He did not begin as a resident at any of the properties; he came into the properties at the recommendation of the American Baptists. He might have been exactly the type of person who didn't fit into Carmen's model of developing residents to manage the properties themselves, but through the strength of his character, and the model that Carmen has integrated into the management of the properties, he has become Carmen's right-hand person and "rock" within the day-to-day operations of the organization. "Keith carries the organization's mission and values in everything he does; he treats the residents with dignity and respect," attests Carmen.

One reason for such longevity and success is, perhaps, that Carmen has created a management culture that gives employees ownership over their positions and the freedom to do the work the way they believe it should be done. Carmen believes in decision-making as close to the point of service as possible. This kind of management is difficult to find.

Carmen also has their back. "No matter what happens," says Carmen, "they know they're supported. No one has definitive answers. We're finding our way together."

These staff represent the best aspects of a fully integrated housing community.

"There's a higher power who guided these people to me, and in that process we've figured out how to help one another," asserts Carmen. "They've created a continuum in the community that I couldn't have fostered in a traditional authoritarian or hierarchical culture."

Ultimately, Carmen could not have succeeded without these dedicated colleagues supporting his mission and the principal values they all share, described by Carmen in this way: "What matters in life is not what you own or possess, but what you give in service to others." In many ways, the individual staff members and their journeys through life have constituted Carmen's own journey. Their compassionate, and at times fierce, devotion to their communities have sustained the programs that provide hope and a way out of the cycle of poverty for many in Madison and Milwaukee.

CHAPTER TWELVE

Family

CARMEN AND MAY LANDED IN MADISON IN 1974. THEY quickly found their respective callings in the community: Carmen in the Northport and Packers communities and May as an early childhood educator at Woodland Montessori School. They joined the First Baptist Church on Franklin Street, where Carmen would occasionally preach and May would teach Sunday school. Separately they pursued their shared social gospel mission, and together they weathered the storm of Carmen's firing and the birth of their three children.

The same sense of purpose that drove Carmen to create housing ministries as a pathway toward social justice drove May to pursue education. May developed a reputation as a particularly compassionate and effective early childhood teacher. "She exemplified a respect and appreciation for children and their ability to teach adults that is rare," says Carmen. He adds that people were often surprised at her patient listening and her awareness of kids' own understanding of their needs and selves. Her teaching was based on the same principles of basic human dignity and high expectations for the potential of people as Carmen's housing management philosophy.

"She worked in early childhood education and getting education that was appropriate for kids to be lifted up and out of their social circumstances," Carmen says.

Montessori education is based on the belief in the capability of children to define their own needs and seek out their own solutions in the classroom. "May's gift was to demonstrate that she believed in you, because you, like her, are capable. Her role as an educator was simply to provide the resources and support," Carmen explains. For Carmen, if housing was to lift people out of the cycle of poverty, it would have to incorporate this notion of education on-site. Together, the couple realized that goal with the construction of community learning centers at the Northport and Packer properties.

"May and I shared some of the similar ideas of what we could do if we built these learning centers on the properties at a time when it was doubtful that we would even survive the housing management of it because things were so bad," Carmen says. "We did it together while starting a family at the same time."

May gave birth to their first child, John, on October 9, 1977. As in Carmen's own birth, the labor and delivery was a long, hard process. Carmen recalls that at one moment, right around the peak of labor, he looked out the window to the stormy sky. A beam of light punched through a small opening in the dark-gray clouds.

"To me, it seemed like that light was coming right from the heavens to shine on us," says Carmen. "The moment felt symbolic, a moment of promise and hope."

Carmen recalls another moment with John when he went to change his first diaper. "It started well enough," Carmen says, but ended badly, with John soaking Carmen in pee. "He looked like he was enjoying every minute of it," Carmen chuckles.

Like many new parents, Carmen and May struggled to adjust to their new roles. John threw tantrums, and the new family sheepishly left restaurants, or were asked to leave. As he grew, John displayed the same stubborn persistence that had seen Carmen through many of the challenges he himself had faced growing up, but the son also demonstrated the deep sensitivity and compassion of his mom. John seemed hell-bent to find his own path; he struggled to stay motivated at school, and after high school, he decided that college wasn't for him.

"He told me not to expect him to go into the ministry, either," says Carmen. The path John took in life wasn't what Carmen would have predicted for him, but over time he saw its value. Like his mom, John was a gifted teacher. He started as a martial arts instructor when he was 16. At 21, he met his future wife, and by the age of 24, he had decided that college was in his future after all. He applied to Grinnell College, where his wife had gone, and he was rejected. He appealed the rejection, soliciting letters from almost 30 parents whose kids he had taught. He was rejected again. John then bargained with the dean of admissions that if he got a 4.0 grade point average over the coming fall at Madison Area Technical College, Grinnell would admit him for spring classes without his having to reapply. The dean agreed.

John did exactly as he had promised, earning a 4.0 in all four classes, and he got into Grinnell.

"He taught me through his actions about his own resilience, that he can channel his anger into positive results," Carmen notes. "I applauded him." Years later, John continued his education, working toward a PhD in education at the University of Wisconsin-Madison.

"He has a strong character," Carmen adds. "And something I like about him is that although he's not going to be in the ministry, he is ministering—he has a passion to make sure kids are not marginalized because of their economic or cultural backgrounds, and his work is about standing up for that, which makes me proud. I know that somewhere May is beaming, too."

May and Carmen's second child, born in 1980, was named Dorothy. Unlike John, Dorothy was social from the get-go.

"When we would go to restaurants, she would seek out anyone who was alone or looked unhappy, then try to engage them and make them laugh or smile," Carmen recalls.

Dorothy was always the hardest worker in the family, often quietly working on her own, then surprising everyone when she emerged to show off what she had accomplished. The summer after she completed first grade, she read voraciously, often completing several-hundred-page books in one sitting. Other things challenged her mightily, though. She worked on her math homework for hours, only to be told that she had arrived at the wrong answer, or had used the wrong problem-solving method.

During her second-grade year, the school tested Dorothy and told her parents that she should be placed in a special education class. Carmen and May felt that the school had based its assessment on incomplete testing, that the school didn't really try to understand Dorothy but instead focused on labeling her. In class, and with her homework, Dorothy would get so frustrated and angry that she couldn't move forward with a particular problem. "It was like a wall was being thrown up between her and the task at hand," recalls Carmen.

When Carmen and May met with school staff, along with the school's attorney, the staff made it clear that they had the ability to act on their assessments without May and Carmen's approval. Carmen had seen the power that schools had to label kids and dictate who they could potentially become. He didn't take kindly to being pushed around, so he and May sought out their own evaluations for Dorothy and committed themselves to supporting her through a different education.

Carmen and May found a psychologist who could form a more complete picture of how Dorothy learned and who helped them locate a school that would work with Dorothy to create strategies for overcoming the challenges she faced in a traditional learning environment.

This new school was expensive, but seeing how hard Dorothy was willing to work to progress, Carmen dedicated himself to finding ways to pay for it. While Dorothy spent countless hours struggling through her homework, honing the strategies she was learning at school to ultimately find success, Carmen volunteered at the school doing odd jobs, painting it after hours, and performing other general labor duties. The school invested in Dorothy, and Carmen wanted to invest in the school. He constantly reminded her that she could "overcome any challenge" and that he was proud of her.

Dorothy was not a traditional learner, but by the end of fifth grade, she was ready to apply herself in a traditional learning environment again. The experience tested Carmen and May, shaking their faith in public schools. Carmen had come to believe that institutions had to prove themselves worthy of the public's trust, but he also believed that people who face the greatest challenges deserve our faith. He continues to carry this skepticism of institutions and faith in people through everything he does in housing. And Dorothy carries this faith in herself.

Carmen recalls Dorothy saying in the sixth grade, "You guys fought for me, and if you hadn't, I wouldn't have had a chance. I won't let you down." Dorothy became the first of Carmen and May's children to graduate from college—and then to earn a master's degree, and then to add a nursing degree. She has traveled the world: from Australia to London, and throughout continental Europe and New Zealand. For a girl who once got lost crisscrossing Madison, she has indeed gone far. For Carmen, Dorothy is living proof that by simply believing in someone, and nurturing their belief in themselves, you can help them overcome incredible obstacles.

The Porcos had no plans to have a third child, but "when we make plans, God often laughs," Carmen chuckles. In 1986, more laughter was added to their lives with an unexpected third child. Margaret's entry into the world was dramatic—she was breech and blue when she emerged, and the doctors had to rush her to intensive care. However, "within 20 minutes she pointed at me and tugged on my beard, and bent her baby finger just like my mother did," remembers Carmen. "I knew from the start that this girl was going to be one tough cookie."

As a child, Margaret showed great stubbornness and determination—not unlike Carmen himself. "God planted her in my life," he says. Perhaps more than her siblings, Margaret has grown to embody Carmen and May's commitment to community.

As the years passed, Carmen and May watched Margaret's character develop more fully. "She's a strong, opinionated person, and when she believes in something, she makes it happen. She goes to bat for others, too. In school, teachers would tell us she was always putting her nose where it didn't belong because she'd defend kids against teachers when she thought the teachers were wrong. Most kids get in trouble at school for being disruptive or making the classroom a worse place; Margaret would get in trouble for arguing to make the classroom fairer," says Carmen.

As a child, Margaret would accompany Carmen to his office, or the properties in Madison and Milwaukee, when she could. She was following in his footsteps. Carmen recalls, "I want to do what you do,' she said to me. She'd worked in the learning centers for years, yes, but I couldn't hire her—she was my daughter!" This was after Margaret had been an intern in Milwaukee and graduated from Lawrence University with a double major in political science and international relations. She had clearly demonstrated her abilities both in the properties and in her work outside of Madison and Milwaukee.

"I think she was inspired by the applications of students for our scholarships, kids who never thought they'd get to go to college and now were able to make the dream real because of our program," Carmen adds.

Carmen encouraged Margaret to find her own path. Margaret spent time working for the Milwaukee and state bar associations but did not feel the same connection to the work that she did when working in the housing properties and kept coming back. She was passionate about the people and mission at Packer, Northport, Greentree, and all the properties that Carmen managed. Carmen's saying that she couldn't work there simply because she was his daughter was not a good enough reason for her. She not only told Carmen so, but she also had set out to show him through her other work in the legal field that she was uniquely prepared and attached to the housing ministry.

"Finally I sent her to the board chair, Roy Nabors. I warned him that hell on wheels was headed his way," says Carmen.

Roy didn't quite understand what Carmen's problem was with hiring her. After talking to Margaret, he said to Carmen, "I think she'll make a great addition to the staff."

That was 10 years ago. She has since worked in various capacities within the organization and now is an assistant director alongside Keith Atchley, set to take over for Carmen when he retires within the next few years. "She has a passion for serving people," Carmen says. "I tell her, 'This is a hard business. Are you sure you want to dedicate your life to it?' And she says yes. I have a great deal of faith and confidence in her leadership. She'll honor the principles at the core of this organization. She's staunch on all of it." While she carries the same passion as Carmen, he believes Margaret is a better collaborator.

As Carmen and May worked to build sustainable communities built on faith in people at Northport and Packer and in Milwaukee, they were challenged time and again to practice a similar faith at home with their children. From John's stubborn refusal to follow a straight path into college or religious studies, to Dorothy's winding road through

America's education institutions, and to Margaret's persistent will to do more, the three offspring all reflect the faith their parents brought to bear at home and in the community as they reshaped housing and education in poor communities.

It wasn't always easy for Carmen to accept and trust the choices his children made, particularly as the kids were younger. John stopped going to church, and Carmen had to trust that he would find his faith outside the traditional church. A cornerstone of the family's Baptist theology was that one must freely give oneself to God. Dorothy was a constant reminder to listen carefully and never presume to know what someone needs, that traditional job training and college prep programs may all be well and good, but also to listen to nontraditional ideas. Finally, Margaret, who came into their life as a late surprise just as they were settling into a happy and complacent routine with the older two children, constantly pushed her parents to do more than they thought they could manage; to grant her more responsibility than they were comfortable with; and to continue with more patience than they thought was warranted to get the job done.

In many ways, the growth of Carmen and May's family mirrored the development of their ministries in housing and education.

CHAPTER THIRTEEN

Housing Ministry

CARMEN AND MAYOR PAUL SOGLIN HAD NOT REMAINED close after their first interaction when Carmen arrived as the new manager of the Northport and Packer properties in Madison. Carmen had written a note when the mayor's father died, sharing his own experience of losing his father and conveying his sympathies, but there wasn't much more to their relationship until 1993, when Carmen invited the mayor to speak at the groundbreaking for the Northport Community Learning Center.

Carmen had changed the institutional framework for providing low-income housing in Madison by changing the way Section 8 funds were administered, getting a property tax exemption from the city, and restructuring the management relationships between the American Baptists and the property residents. He had hired and trained residents for property management positions and had created management documents and processes that honored the dignity of residents and outlined the shared responsibility of everyone in the community.

Over the years, the staff and residents at Northport and Packer had grown and thrived together, and their hard work had paid off. They had constructed community learning centers at each site. The ground-breaking events were well attended by residents and members of the community, and the mayor spoke graciously and with great confidence about the new endeavor.

Two months later, Carmen invited Mayor Soglin to Packer for an open house so he could see the centers in action. Often housing programs, like churches ministries, are too focused on the physical spaces and places as they envision success; Carmen wanted the mayor to also see the people and actions that had made Northport and Packer into model communities. The mayor was impressed, and this time Carmen took the opportunity to remind him that he didn't need an invitation to visit the communities and was welcome anytime. Their relationship had come a long way since Mayor Soglin had called Carmen "the biggest scum lord of them all."

Six months later, Carmen received a call from Pat Wongkit, Northport's program coordinator. She thought that she had missed an appointment or meeting notice. The mayor was on the grounds, and he had brought two alderpersons with him. Carmen reassured Pat that there was no formal meeting and that she should give the mayor and the alderpersons a tour of the complex and otherwise go about her normal routine.

The next morning, Carmen received a call from the mayor and an invitation to join him in Los Angeles at the U.S. Conference of Mayors. Carmen accepted, excited at the chance to spread the word about his housing management model among people with a nation-wide influence.

At the conference, Carmen got the chance to talk about his model with both the secretary of HUD and the secretary of the Department of Education. Federal officials were impressed with Carmen's learning centers. Later, Education Secretary Richard Riley sought $40 million from Congress to create Community Learning Centers of the 21st

Century for public schools, and Henry Cisneros, the HUD secretary, put together a comparable model of Neighborhood Networks for public housing, based in part on Carmen's model. Carmen's hope to effect national change was realized only marginally, however, because the federal models fell short of adopting Carmen's model, which provided a whole array of services to residents ranging from child care to job placement. Carmen may not have gotten his housing management model adopted, but the conference did strengthen his relationship with the mayor even more.

"I hadn't realized it at the time, but the mayor and I had become allies in the cause of social justice," says Carmen. "We never discussed it, but after that conference we had a deeper respect for each other."

After Mayor Soglin returned to private life, he founded a consultancy called The Rising Tide, to study how success can spread from community to community. He and Carmen began a habit of meeting occasionally for breakfast to discuss their similar initiatives and interests. For the most part, they discussed Madison's social and economic challenges. At their meetings, Carmen often talked about the core tenants of his model and his belief that society's problems with poverty reflect its inability to trust or respect the underclass and provide an institutional framework that gives poor people the chance to make decisions, define the problems, and create solutions.

"He showed a great deal of concern about injustice and how to make a system that doesn't let people drop out when they don't feel a part of it, like welfare," says Carmen. "The mayor liked that my model was integrated, that it requires people of all backgrounds to understand that their success is mutually dependent, that we believed in hiring residents for jobs and supporting their success, and that we focus on education as a way to break the chain of poverty."

The two men's backgrounds are different—Soglin was a lawyer and a politician, Carmen a theologian—but they are both still heavily influenced by the anti-institutionalism that drove them into their careers back in the 1960s. In a way, that terrible first meeting between the two might have been a happy accident, Carmen says, because it immediately revealed each man's strengths and flaws. Both men are hard-headed, aggressive, tenacious leaders with a passion for equality and justice for the poor. They have each come a long way from that first contentious meeting. Carmen has come to admire the former mayor, and Soglin has become a great proponent of Carmen's housing management model. "I really respect him, and he respects me, too," says Carmen.

———

One of the first things Carmen did in developing his model was to train his management team to incorporate human rights and due process into the management model. This shift would not only focus the staff on the human dignity of the residents, but it would give the residents a seat at the table in a mutual relationship. The idea was to counter the inherent power differential that benefits landlords in our legal system. "We created a management concept that honored the people," Carmen says. "The first principle was redefining housing management, and that definition went something like, 'Housing management is the art of integrating and coordinating human and technical resources to establish the potential of a human community, not just property.'

"In order for that definition to have integrity, we needed to hire residents for the jobs created by the property management, and also integrate human services under one legal organizational structure, instead of human services being offered by outside groups and the owners doing all the management. I wanted the management of the property and the human services to be one integrated delivery system."

It's one thing to say that residents deserve respect and another to demonstrate this respect in a concrete way. Carmen wanted residents to be certain from the start that their needs were being considered and their voices heard. When he first took on the job of directing property management there was nothing in the resident leases about the owner's responsibility to the people served.

"How can we include human rights in the leases?" Carmen asked his staff.

A lease with a stated unified responsibility—owner and manager and resident—along with a new orientation manual that highlighted how residents' interests were protected in the lease arrangement, was needed. This was a complicated challenge because HUD requires certain aspects of this relationship to be spelled out in particular ways. Carmen set about creating a document in addition to the lease that put his values in action.

"We aimed to end the psychology of residents feeling like they have no decision-making power," states Carmen. "Not all the power was in the hands of the managers, and the residents could feel that. If there was a conflict with a resident, we didn't evict based on property rights; we gave the resident a chance to work it out legally. When word got around that this was how we operated, there were fewer conflicts overall."

To Carmen's delight, those staff members who were themselves low-income residents understood instinctively how the new relationship benefited them. "They had experience with systems that put them in unequal positions," says Carmen, "so it was easy for them to imagine an equal system and work for it. They embraced the changes."

Another prime example of how Carmen's philosophy impacted housing is how evictions are now handled on two different levels. The first is how late payment is handled; the second is the subjective nature of evictions.

Within one to two generations, Milwaukee had gone from being one of the best places in America for African-American families because of the preponderance of well-paying blue-collar jobs to one of the worst as those jobs disappeared to the suburbs and were replaced by low-paying service jobs or jobs that required high degrees of education. For many, money was tight. The American financial system is set up so that it is expensive to live if you don't have money and cheaper the more money you have. People with more money get lower interest rates on loans or higher interest returns on their savings, while people with less money have to pay more to borrow, or pay late fees. The system judges your human value by the size of your bank account. Carmen saw this as one way that poverty reproduces itself, and he worked through his management systems to try insert greater fairness in the process.

"When people were late for rent, I noticed that some people didn't get a notice," Carmen says about the old system. "And when others did get a notice, it was eviction. So we said, no, there are a couple of ways that we are changing this. First of all, if rent is due on the fifth of the month or the seventh of the month, if the person came in before that deadline and said that they were having trouble paying, we could work out an agreement with them and they wouldn't get a notice. If the person did not come in before the deadline, they would get the first notice that said they had a chance to correct their late rent. You could have two late periods in a period of 12 months and not have a problem. But if you didn't come in and you had two late periods and then the third time you didn't come in at all, you would get a 14-day notice, which said that we were going to let a judge decide." This was all explained in terms of mutual respect. If the residents respect the staff enough to talk with them, then the staff can work with them. Even if a resident got a 14-day notice, Carmen and his staff would show empathy, going an extra mile with them.

"A lot of times we would say to our attorney, 'If their attorney is trying to be reasonable and willing to get the client in shape, we will work with them and not go to court,'" Carmen says. "We extended the rule by saying it has to be formal and it has to be applied consistently across the board. There is a grace period if they show accountability in coming in. Even the first notice is not an eviction notice. It's a 10-day notice of correction. In other words, we're putting it on record legally that if they don't come in during that 10-day period, then we have no option but go to court."

Before Carmen came to Wisconsin, evictions could be baseless. "In some cases, the reason for eviction was shallow," Carmen emphasized. "For example, if, in Milwaukee, you were white and a black family moved in—each hallway had four units—if the three white folks wrote a complaint about the black person, the management would institute a legal action. Our process said, 'No, that's not respecting human rights.' If three people write a letter to get one person out, our first attempt is to try to get the people together to discuss it and come to resolution. In the case that all three would say, 'No this person is wrong,' I would listen to them carefully and I would say to them, 'We're not here to take sides. We're here to try to reconcile things. But if you aren't willing to reconcile, then I have a notice for every one of you.' When word got around that I would empty the units, that stuff stopped.

"We're going to do a legal process that has the foundation of human rights. Due process has to be in place that protects their interests. It also helped me to help managers understand that it's not personality or personal. You are representing an organization. The lease is not between you and the resident. It's between the resident and the organization you work for. You have to broker a win-win for both. That's how we changed the eviction process."

Through the staff training, leasing, orientation, and eviction processes, staff learned to change the binary management–resident power relationship. Carmen encouraged his staff to think about not just that power imbalance but the impacts of their actions on everyone.

"We're mandated to create a system that puts all parties on an equal level and allows no party to gain at the detriment of another party. We needed to change who got the management jobs and put a structure in place that would change the power relationships. Residents needed to occupy the maintenance, management, administrative, and program management positions," explains Carmen.

In Carmen's vision, all parties touched by the community are clients, including the property owners, HUD, stockholders on the profit side, the management company, the residents, the taxpayer, and even citizens of the greater area. In an effective management culture, all clients are served and no one party's interests are leveraged against another's. Profit-motivated owners can't generate cash, for example, without considering the ramifications to the residents themselves. In a holistic, client-centered housing management system, Carmen feels that everybody wins.

After getting the leases and manuals into shape, Carmen and his staff tackled the new resident orientation program. In the system they developed, new residents aren't asked simply to sign a lease but are also oriented in a way that introduces them to the rights and responsibilities of the community. This includes a meeting with the manager to go over all the documents in terms of mutual responsibilities, a review of the resident manual that outlines the resident rights and responsibilities and a tour and an in-depth introduction to all opportunities and services offered on-site with the program coordinators. These opportunities are what make Carmen's model unique: services like childcare and Head Start, afterschool programs, college preparatory programs, adult education programs, and employment assistance programs, as well as summer programs like field trips, art and crafts, filmmaking classes, and science programs.

This comprehensive orientation is meant not only to clarify the resident's responsibilities as a new member of the community but also to clarify the responsibilities of the staff and management to the residents and the avenues of recourse available to residents if problems should arise. The orientation emphasizes that the community is not a one-sided contract governed by a lease document but, rather, a partnership between staff, management, and residents. Often the program coordinators become advocates for the children at school and families in their communities when problems arise.

More challenging for Carmen than training his staff, however, was establishing working relationships with the service providers that came into the community. These outside vendors had to be trained to understand the core values and respect for human dignity at the center of Carmen's model in order to abide by them. Sometimes this training was beyond Carmen's control. Sometimes external service providers were asked to go through similar orientation processes as the residents. Sometimes they would not be allowed to offer services in the community because they were not willing to do so in a way that honored the residents, the mission, or the values.

"As I experienced it through the years, I was angered by the fact that a social worker here in Wisconsin could go in, visit a woman with children, and threaten her with loss of services. One lady asked me to be there when the social worker came. I witnessed a social worker opening a woman's drawers and finding men's clothing, then questioning the woman about them," recounts Carmen.

"Just think about how demeaning and threatening such behavior is," he adds. "Social workers sanctioned by the state are enforcing policies that result in separating children from their fathers by keeping the man out of the house. If women receiving assistance don't comply with these rules, they face a loss of benefits that could end up decimating their families even more.

"I told the social worker she didn't have a right to do that, to invade her privacy. Then with my friend's permission, I threw the social worker out and went to see her supervisor. The supervisor was kind, but she told me I was wrong, that the social worker had a right to do what she did. So I started to study social programs, and I realized that these programs destroyed African-American families, removed the African-American male from the family unit and made sure he had no place.

"When I give sermons, sometimes I use that example and say that we didn't realize that America had such a widespread example of divine conception—all these African-American ladies with children and no men involved. I just wished I was smarter and knew how to better challenge the system that is still in place today."

Carmen started by building program capacity within the community first and by not relying on any outside providers or funding. Once that was successful, he carefully selected partners based on shared values, and he worked with those who respected the dignity of the residents when they came on-site. This could be a constant struggle with new social workers and inspectors coming through all the time. That's when the staff training played a central role in their standing up for the residents when appropriate.

"The War on Poverty is like any war we declare—we don't care who we kill in the process. It's the fundamental error in logic of the War on Poverty. When we give people control over the jobs, the resources, and the responsibility of naming the problems and coming up with the solutions, then, and only then, can people pull themselves out of poverty," Carmen says.

In his experience, mainstream institutions were not as comfortable providing low-income communities with educational services as they were with providing athletic services. His message has always been, "We don't just hand out basketballs. The greatest muscle to develop is the mind. Your mental power will see you farther than your athletic power. A ball player might be a star for a while, and then disappear into the dustbin of history. They can never steal your mind."

One of Carmen's most daunting challenges was how to ensure that his model was self-sufficient and sustainable, and to keep it funded by a portion of rent paid by residents, since government programs can be reduced or cut at any time. He addressed that challenge by designing a budget that escrows monies into a permanent account to fund programs, services, and staffing. Carmen also created a fund for educational scholarships, which over time has awarded nearly $1 million to more than 227 residents for advanced education. Although it took him many years and appeals, he finally convinced HUD in 1989 to allow him to use federal funds to implement his educational and community development ideas. Over time, that money served as the capital needed for the construction not just of the buildings, but of the opportunities that the community needed.

Construction began on community learning centers at Carmen's Madison properties in 1993 and 1994 and at the Milwaukee properties in 1997 and 1998. For 10 years, Carmen had escrowed the property tax savings because these funds would allow him to build the community learning centers without taking out loans.

Later, HUD would call its version of Carmen's educational centers Neighborhood Networks; there are now more than 1,000 such centers in housing sites across the country. Carmen resisted HUD's branding of the services, which emphasized the computer offerings over the human and educational component. Carmen's facilities provided access to a network, yes, but they were also concerned with educational opportunities, skill development, and community development. They were much more than what was reflected in HUD's Neighborhood Networks.

Neighborhood Networks were the result of HUD's development of a program for the digital age that Al Gore had pushed. As part of the program, every low-income housing development was to have Internet computer capacity. The Neighborhood Networks were never intended to be an actual community-type service center as much as they were intended to just be a digital hub. There were thoughts that every apartment would be wired and everyone would have free Internet access. In the process of trying to develop the program, HUD started with community centers that had computers and called them Neighborhood Networks—this was not a funded program but, rather, a symbolic gesture of concept. Carmen's community learning centers are about more than technology. In his centers, technology is a way to access education or skill development rather than being the central thrust of the centers. That's why Carmen called his complexes community learning centers.

"We were the first ones who opened a community learning center in a low-income housing development. And we are the longest, consistently running Neighborhood Network. The program, for the most part, is not even mentioned anymore at HUD. It was about digital access and not education," Carmen explains.

While having digital access was important to provide tools for the communities at Northport and Packer, and the investment in high-end equipment spoke volumes to the residents about their worth, the computer centers were only the beginning of a system that provided the opportunity for hope to Carmen's residents.

The success of Carmen's model is heavily supported by the data. Throughout the 805 housing units in Madison and Milwaukee where Carmen's model is at work, high school graduation rates approach 100 percent, and more than 75 percent of high school graduates go on to higher education. This has held true for most of the twenty-first century. Over 50 residents are fully employed and making a living wage on-site and have been in their posts for 10 years or longer, which gives the communities a remarkable degree of stability. Crime rates in the communities are some of the lowest in their cities.

In the nearly 30 years since Carmen started implementing his model, thousands of people's careers, families, and lives have improved significantly.

Three times a year, the communities award thousands of dollars in scholarships to a competitive group of young people, and some kids who have graduated through those scholarships return to volunteer at the community learning centers and keep other kids involved.

Perhaps the true potential of Carmen's housing ministry is conveyed not by the data but in the words of staff, residents, and former residents.

"This model not only impacted my personal life," says Jacki Thomas, "it became the lens through which I view the world. I am convinced that the successes I have witnessed are primarily attributed to each individual's effort, integrity, and merit, but I recognize that it would have been nearly impossible without stable housing, a space where community can develop as a support system, and clear-eyed believers in the value of each individual."

Pat Wongkit, says, "I am who I am today because of what I've learned from Carmen and his model. I believe in it wholeheartedly. It made me see how people can actually develop if you believe in them and give them the resources they need. This place makes me feel so proud of what we do, what we believe in. I'll retire from here if they will have me that long."

Beyond the devout belief in this system apparent in the staff, testimony from the residents reveals the authentic nature of the community and the opportunities it provides. Omari, age 10, says of his community, "I get help with my homework, and I have nice neighbors. The lady across the hall says if she plays the music too loud, just knock on her door and she will turn it down. But it's never too loud. No one smokes in our building, and that's good because my sister has asthma."

Jessica moved to Northport when she was 18 and remained a resident for six years. "As a young mother on my own, I found Northport Apartments vital to my independence today," she says. "I felt a strong sense of community. I was there for the community learning center construction and watched my neighborhood develop. The staff played a vital role in the success of the residents. Computer classes and resume and job-seeking assistance aided many people to obtain a better life."

Ashley Suarez grew up in the Northport Apartments. "Northport has helped my family in so many ways! I am so grateful for having had the opportunity to live there," she says. "The learning center offered so many activities for us as kids growing up in the neighborhood. It really helped my mother, being a single parent; she had extra hands to help us. I wouldn't change where I grew up. I learned so many things, and I know Northport was always there for me and my family."

About the Greentree complex, an unidentified resident says, "Greentree gives opportunity to everyone, no matter their circumstances. They can get a fresh start here."

Perhaps Jacki Thomas sums it up best: "Porco's housing units are places where it is possible to find someone to believe in you for the long haul. Some of our best success stories are those that came after multiple trials. This is a very good place to find yourself if you are feeling alone in school or the larger world. We provide a clearinghouse for information, a network of personal introductions to outside resources, and best of all, a review system taking into account the past experiences of others with outside agencies."

As Carmen enters the last phase of his career as a minister and as a leader, he finds himself reflecting on what he's accomplished—and where he's fallen short of his goals. "I don't think I've been as effective as I needed to be in promoting the accomplishments of my model, showing the larger world what those accomplishments could mean for our society," he reflects.

Carmen considers what might happen if HUD were to fully transform according to the principles he's tested and proven—from an organization that merely provides shelter to one that rebuilds human dignity, gives residents jobs, provides educational opportunities within the community, and recycles rental income back into scholarships and career development for residents. "With HUD's reach, whole communities could be pulled from poverty toward opportunity; what a huge difference that could make," he says.

When Carmen looks at his own developments, he feels a strong sense of pride that his housing communities don't have the problems of high rates of teen pregnancy and drug use that others do and that his residents stay more than 10 years on average. His pride is tempered by doubt that HUD will take up the model nationally.

That said, he's hopeful that his housing ministry model will propagate organically, as those who benefit from it—like Pat, Vickie, and Jackie—have shared the example of their leadership to a new generation of neighborhood kids, interns, and community members.

Already the next generation of these individuals who grew up in and around this model are stepping into leadership positions. Martinus Roper, a resident in Milwaukee, is working as Vicki's assistant program coordinator and brings his own ideas to program development. Pat has another assistant who grew up at Northport, obtained a master's degree, and has come back because she feels her heart remains in the Northport community and she wants to give back. Jacki's daughter served as her assistant and then the interim program coordinator until one of her former student interns took the job, at which point she went on to finish her graphic design degree and launch her own career. Carmen's daughter, Margaret, has taken over handling rent negotiations with HUD and the development of values-based policies for the organization. All of these individuals that are being groomed for leadership are a final testament to not only the success of Carmen's model but its sustainability.

The impressive computer labs, community learning center buildings, and countless awards Carmen has received mark the success of his housing ministry. The accomplishments of his staff, the hundreds of scholarships awarded, the changed lives, and the hope that has been expressed by property residents speak volumes about his original vision.

Carmen recently received a text message from Pat, who had been awarded one of President Obama's volunteerism and community awards. "Did you do this?" asked Pat. Out in front of the Northport development, workers were stringing Christmas lights through the trees. At night, they lit up the whole street between Northport and Packer. Carmen had wanted it to be a surprise. In truth, the whole community had made it possible. "All the children are smiling," wrote Pat.

"Makes all these years worth it," Carmen wrote back.

CHAPTER FOURTEEN

Heartbroken

MAY WOULD HAVE LOVED THOSE CHRISTMAS LIGHTS along Northport Avenue, but more than that, she would have loved to see the smiles on all the children's faces." From their marriage in her childhood backyard in 1971; from their adventures around the country to the incorporation of educational programs at the community learning centers, May had been by Carmen's side for 43 years.

May 12, 2013, was Mother's Day. The whole family headed out to brunch at Captain Bill's in Middleton because they had raw cookie dough as a part of the buffet—you could just get ice cream scoops full of it. It was a beautiful sunny day; the light glimmered off the lake. Everyone feasted and celebrated all the moms, but mostly May. May didn't feel much like eating, however. Her stomach just felt a little off. The next week she went in to the doctor, and after a battery of tests, her doctor confirmed that she had pancreatic cancer.

The doctors hoped they had caught it soon enough that they could shrink it and operate on it, but pancreatic cancer is almost always fatal. Surgery was not immediately an option because the tumor was abutting her aorta. She began chemotherapy in June.

Carmen felt his world falling apart. Everything he had built and worked for had been with May, and now he was finally ready to move into retirement and start a new chapter with her. He was not ready to lose his wife, and he was angry. May kept him from getting bitter. "Let's just make the most of the time we have," she said to him. They spent more time going to antique shops, and they started looking for a lake house on Lake Michigan.

May was not the type to have a "bucket list," Carmen recalls, but she had quietly longed for a small lake house or cottage because some of her fondest memories were of bonding with family and friends at her family's cottage as a child. When May was growing up, her family had a cottage on the beach, and her best friend's family also had a beach cottage south of Boston. She hoped her own family, which by then included three grandkids with a fourth coming soon, would be able to bond and make similar memories there.

Carmen found that the stress of dealing with the cancer eased slightly because of the distraction in looking for a cottage. They looked high and low for a lake house in their budget range and found nothing. Then they went with a real estate agent to see a place that belonged to an older gentleman—a widower—who was moving into a condo. While May and the kids looked through the house, Carmen sat with the man, talking.

"I felt like looking at the house was tantamount to prearranging a funeral," says Carmen. "But this man and I had something in common; he had lost his wife, and I was going to lose mine."

During the course of their conversation, the man asked Carmen about his plans for the house, if he were to buy it. Would he tear it down to build a bigger house like everyone else on the lake? No, Carmen told him, "this house is solid. We'd keep it." The man asked Carmen what he could afford, and Carmen gave him a number. "Too low," said the man. "Add $5,000." Carmen agreed, and they shook hands. The deal was done.

"Here we'd been looking for weeks and not able to afford anything, but then this giant four-bedroom house comes up, with 3,500 square feet and three fireplaces, right on Lake Michigan, and May's dream became a reality," concludes Carmen.

Over the next year, the family found ways to spend time together, both at home and at the lake. They planned one last trip with May to Disney World. Every celebration took on new significance: birthdays, holidays, etc. The family spent their first Christmas at the lake house— May's last. It was amazing how May's uplifting spirit dominated these events, holding the impending sadness at bay until she went to sleep at night. At home she would often be tired, either from the chemo or just being sick. At the lake, she found energy to host a tea party with her grandkids, set up a table to sketch at while looking out over the lake, or walk out to the edge of the bluff to have a sit. May would wake up early to watch the sunrise and listen to the waves—perhaps reminiscing back to her childhood. For most of the family, the only strength they had over those final 16 months came from May.

In July 2014, May's fourth grandchild was born. May had fought so hard to be able to be there for this new person. She was the first family member to meet the new baby. Carmen wheeled her into the hospital room at 5:00 a.m. She beamed as she welcomed that baby with the same grace and warmth she had given to all her kids and grandkids, despite the enormous toll the cancer had taken on her. She had taken as much radiation as a person is allowed in a lifetime, and she had gone through over 12 months of intense chemotherapy. She spent one more month giving her family, particularly her grandchildren, the same smiles and playfulness that had defined her work at the Montessori school, and with Carmen's staff.

"She didn't really have to prepare for the end," Carmen says. "Her God was always with her, and she had an unyielding faith." On August 15, May told Carmen it was time to go to the hospital. He and May lived at the hospital until she was discharged to hospice care for her final few days.

"Throughout that time, she remained very positive, encouraging everyone to move forward," Carmen recalls. "Two days before she died, she talked to me alone. She told me she'd treasured our loving relationship and she wanted me to find someone to have as a new partner so I'm not alone in life; that would make her happy. She attempted to insert a little humor by saying that she had one condition: 'Just make sure she has more money than me.'"

Carmen never left May's side. Going to all the doctor appointments, staying up through the night when she was really sick, and during the difficult last weeks and hours of May's life, Carmen wiped her mouth and her forehead with a cool cloth. Intermittently, he paused to wipe the tears from his own eyes. He told her it was all right to let go, that she had done enough. During the day of August 28, 2014, May had a chance to talk to each of her family members and close friends to say good-bye. That night, the family gathered around, played music, and ate pizza. Quietly she passed into the night. She had planned her own funeral and left instructions for her remains. She was to be cremated, with her ashes scattered in various places that were meaningful to her and her kids.

At the memorial, they passed out boxes wrapped in a green ribbon—May's favorite color. These boxes were intended to convey the meaning of one's life journey on earth: that we come into the world empty and fill ourselves as we grow and experience only to pass everything along so that we are empty again when we return to God. The family made 750 boxes and were still 12 short. May had planned a beautiful service, but it wasn't for her. It was for the people she cared about.

Family spoke of the sparkles and glimmers of joy they continued to find because of her memory; they read poems and played jazz on the clarinet in outbursts of emotion that were sad, happy, or joyful. Friends from the Montessori school sang her favorite songs, and others offered comfort, including Mayor Paul Soglin. "The mayor's speech came straight from the heart. He acknowledged May's inclusive compassion. It was a speech of great substance," Carmen recalls. "It meant the world to me."

"Her memorial was about remembering that she was a person of character, a great love, and that she had dedicated her life to protecting children," Carmen adds.

Carmen fell into a deep depression after May's passing. The grief from her death seemed insurmountable at times, and he sought support and counsel from his family and trusted friends. Daughter Margaret and her husband, Bryan, moved in with him. Son John called regularly, and they enjoyed nighttime cigars and fellowship together. This was also a time for Carmen to reflect and reminisce.

Old Friends

In addition to the support of his family, Carmen leaned on long-time friends to help carry him through this hard time. Some of these friends, like George Fleming, Roy Nabors, and Everett Mitchell, had worked with Carmen and May throughout the years as part of his housing developments.

While Carmen's children did most of the day-to-day work of lifting Carmen's spirit, his longtime friend George Fleming also did a lot of heavy lifting. George had grown up on a cotton plantation in Clarksdale, Mississippi, and after moving to Chicago, where he met his wife, the couple relocated to Madison long before Carmen did.

In 1981, when HUD asked Carmen to take over Bram Hill Apartments, a housing development on Madison's south side, they told him that the maintenance guy, George Fleming, was interested in staying on. That was the beginning of a 38-year friendship between the two men. Carmen recalls the start of their relationship like this:

"So I gave George a call, and he and I met up at a restaurant to get to know each other a bit. After we'd talked for a while, I asked if he'd work with me to turn the place around. George hesitated when I asked him to become my partner because he wasn't sure if I could handle the job, since I was white and most of the residents at the complex were 'angry and black,' as he put it. I told him about my childhood, growing up in the barroom in Weirton, and I told him I was pretty sure I could handle it.

"He and I did the physical work of restoring the complex, rolling sod and planting grass, replacing windows, putting in brick patios, fixing the plumbing, and adjusting the hot water heaters. Whatever came up, we got it resolved." As the two men worked together, they talked and got to know one another.

"George shared a lot about what it's like to work a cotton field — It's hot! He and I talked about Reverend Martin Luther King, and he told me with pride that he'd gone to hear the reverend speak at a church in Clarksdale," Carmen says. "He'd been inspired and had come away believing things would change. We discussed equality everywhere we went, and it related to almost everything we did together, including addressing the harassment residents received from police officers."

"George is a man of great character," adds Carmen. A story Carmen likes to share about George is when he bought an extension chain saw so neither of them would have to climb a ladder when the trees needed trimming. It was a 16-foot extension and a pretty pricey piece of equipment. One day, a friend of George's saw him using it and asked to borrow it. George agreed and told his friend to bring it back—but his friend never returned it. George went around to collect it, and the friend said it had been stolen and that's it.

"If it had been me, I'd have come back and reported that the chain saw had been stolen, and that would be that," Carmen says, but that wasn't George. "Instead, he went out and bought another and returned it to me. I told him no, we'll return it; our insurance will pay for it, and I'll replace it. But he was adamant that it was his responsibility. I don't know many people with that level of integrity. It's unique."

Over time, George revealed himself to be a strong person in other ways as well, and their friendship thrived. Carmen says people who come in contact with George feel like they know him well, just like they are known by him. He was nicknamed by many the Mayor of the South Side.

"People always say they wish they could be as calm as George," Carmen recalls. "Once, I asked George where he got his calm patience, and he said, 'Long suffering.'"

It took George many years to feel the freedom of speech and thought without fear of repercussion, even death.

When they started working together, George was in his 30s and Carmen was in his 20s. "George had been deeply scarred by racism long before, and he saw me as a boss first and foremost. I was the first person who ever said to him, 'That's a good idea. Let's do it your way.' When over the years I've taken him to fundraisers and political events, he's fit in equally with the highest income levels and the lowest income levels," says Carmen.

Years later, George met Carmen's brother Cheech, who had heard all about George when the brothers caught up by telephone.

"Cheech and George were instant friends, I think because they both had the biggest hands I'd ever seen," Carmen recalls. "As soon as they shook, they couldn't believe their eyes. They had an easy camaraderie. Later, when George was in Pennsylvania, he stayed the night with Cheech, and they had dinner and got to know each other better."

George was so easy to talk to, he could have been a counselor. When people divulged their troubles to him, he was always receptive and wise.

"After I lost my mother, he would check on me from time to time, whereas most people moved on after a week or so. Even a year later, he was asking how I was doing with the loss. When he lost his own mother, I did the same. Not because I was obligated, but because he'd become my brother," Carmen says proudly.

When Carmen lost his last brother, Cheech, George came to the house, and they sat and talked and cried.

"I felt I still had one brother on earth," Carmen says. "He has helped me on more levels than most people ever could. And he's an interesting soul, a quiet person walking in our midst who has the strength to help a person through any depth of anxiety. We trust each other and call each other brothers. If you asked him, he'd say the same."

After May's passing, George helped Carmen to cope. "He was there for me at my most difficult moments. He reminded me of all the great times we had together," Carmen says.

At the Bram Hill Apartments, they had an old tractor with no cab, and one wintery day Carmen came outside and asked to take a spell at driving it so that George could take a break. Carmen recounts what happened next:

"George went to get coffee while I plowed snow, and it took the longest time and I was freezing, because back then I liked the cold weather and I wore only a lightweight coat and no gloves or hat. But this time it was freezing snow, and I was trying to hurry. There was only one place on the property where it was possible to get stuck, and sure enough I got stuck there. I decided to try to stay warm and sat on the engine. George showed up and took one look at me and started laughing. There were icicles in my hair and beard."

George helped Carmen down from his perch, and they sat in George's truck with the heater going, drinking coffee and swapping stories.

George worked for Carmen from 1981 until he retired in 2016. He helped Carmen find someone to replace him, but then he realized retirement wasn't his thing, so today he's back on the payroll.

"All those years, he had my back, and he gave 150 percent. I figure he's banked credit with me, and I'll continue to pay him as long as I own the property, whether he works a lot or not at all," vows Carmen.

Another kindred spirit who has been with Carmen throughout the years, and even more so after May passed, is Roy Nabors. Carmen met Roy Nabors in 1974, only three weeks after Carmen arrived in Wisconsin. Roy, an inner-city pastor, was trying to build low-income housing units, and he had been turned away by HUD at the national level and WHEDA (Wisconsin Housing and Economic Development Society) at the state level. Roy was advised by those organizations to reach out to the American Baptists because the organization had experience developing low-income housing. Carmen was Roy's point of contact for the American Baptists at his new job with the National Housing Ministries.

"I told Roy, 'Hey, I've only been here three weeks, and we have some really serious problems, so I'm not sure I'm any help to anyone, but let's meet and see how it goes," recalls Carmen.

At their meeting, Carmen recognized a kindred spirit in Roy, a passion for living the gospel and serving the needs of people," as Carmen puts it. "It was refreshing to see a pastor in the inner city who made faith come alive through his own resilience and humility," says Carmen. "I knew I wanted to help."

Carmen looked up the Milwaukee number for Congressman Henry Reuss's office, called the number, and asked to speak to the congressman. The voice on the other end of the line said, "The congressman is speaking."

For a minute, Carmen was stunned into silence. But he looked across the desk at his new friend and colleague, Roy Nabors, and summoned the confidence to speak. He and the congressman set up a meeting, and eventually the congressman went to bat for Roy. Carmen went with Roy and two lay people in Roy's church, Fairbanks Cooper and Dr. Trinette V. McCray, to Washington, D.C. They met with Congressman Reuss and his aides, as well as with HUD officials. Within four weeks, HUD had committed to help fund the building of Calvary Gardens Apartments, a 94-unit elderly housing development in Milwaukee next to Roy's church and a key part of Roy's vision.

Laughs Carmen, "I'll never forget Roy saying to me, 'You've been here three weeks, and you have the congressman wrapped around your finger. I hate to see what you'll have wrapped around your finger in a year.'"

The friendship grew deeper from that point on. The two men shared a similar background. Carmen and Roy met regularly over the years to talk about theology and justice. They shared similar values and perspectives on the church and saw eye-to-eye on changes in the church: how it was wobbling in its prophetic role of serving the poor and not training ministers the way it used to.

"Each of Roy's breaths was dedicated to gospel justice," says Carmen, "and there was no ego in Roy demanding attention for himself. He was in full submission to God's will and glory."

Before building the learning centers in Madison and Milwaukee, amid rumors that HUD funding would be slashed by then-President Reagan, Carmen invited Roy to join his board of directors. Roy initially declined, saying he was already on too many boards, but Carmen persisted, and once Roy was on the board, he quickly assumed the position of chair. Building a board that was ideologically aligned was an important part of the institutional change that Carmen brought to the properties in Madison and Milwaukee. Roy was integral in the battle to build the learning centers. After building the centers, Roy said to Carmen, "That was too easy. Next let's do something hard."

When Carmen proposed to the board that they escrow excess funds to use for scholarships, Roy waited for the other board members to discuss the pros and cons. When it was his turn to weigh in, he invoked a higher consciousness about the purpose of the business—to improve the lives of people in poverty through employment and education—thus shifting the discussion and winning approval of the scholarships.

"With sound theological framing, he'd remind us all that we weren't a real estate group, not primarily. We're a faith-based community, and our actions must speak louder than our words," explains Carmen. When Roy retired, the Milwaukee developments named their scholarships after him: the Roy B. Nabors Scholarship Fund, which continues to award scholarships in his name.

The two colleagues and friends talked frequently after May's passing. Their mutual admiration and affection continues to this day. They like to get together to smoke pipes; Roy's tobacco is some of the strongest Carmen's ever tasted. At lunch not too long ago, at an African-American restaurant where Roy had taken Carmen to see if Carmen would eat chitlins—he did! All during a discussion about commonality and segregation.

In 2017, Carmen returned to Roy's church in Milwaukee for a tribute, and Roy took to the pulpit again.

"I'll tell you," says Carmen, "the man can preach. He puts together the stepping-stones that make you want to scale the highest mountain. Hearing him preach—it's a gift."

Today, Roy is retired and living in St. Louis and mentoring a small church that's grown enormously under his leadership. On the phone with Carmen, he talks with passion about his work. "Retirement's not really in my psyche," says Roy.

Roy is now dealing with the loss of his wife, Betty, and Carmen has reached out to his dear friend in sympathy. Roy spoke eloquently and lovingly at May's funeral and helped Carmen get through his grief, and now Carmen is trying hard to return that kindness.

While both George and Roy offered Carmen the quiet council of friendship after May's passing, Everett Mitchell has been a warm reminder that the work for social justice must continue.

It's been less than 10 years since Everett Mitchell came to Madison. He and Carmen met through friends who thought Carmen would be a good connection since they'd both been to theological seminary and Everett didn't know many people in town at that time.

"The first time we spoke, I teased him about going to a second-rate seminary—he went to Princeton—and he surprised me when he told me he'd had one of my professors, Max Stackhouse, who had been tremendously important to me at Andover-Newton. We agreed that although Max had been a little difficult to understand, since he spoke almost exclusively in very big words, he'd been a great theologian."

Everett and Carmen also talked that first time about what Everett wanted to do with his life. Everett shared with Carmen the great deal of anger he felt about growing up in the South, having experienced racism firsthand, directly and deeply.

"His mother had guided him through those situations, and so had a deacon at the local church," says Carmen, recalling his own anger and the faith that Dave Stone and others had had in him that had channeled that anger toward positive change. "After I got a handle on the kind of anger he was dealing with, I asked Everett to be an intern for us, if for no other reason than to work on gathering power that's spiritually based rather than originating with anger.

"I asked Everett to transform people by embracing the unlovable and doing as Dr. King taught us, by remembering that love is the only force that can turn an enemy into a friend."

Carmen and Everett had great discussions, and they often disagreed.

"He used to tell me I was just a typical white guy. If I hadn't loved him, I would have turned my back to him—but I was trying to model my own advice," says Carmen.

When Everett was an intern, Carmen witnessed Everett as a deeply dedicated individual who had a passion for justice and keen ability to interpret Christianity as the sum of words and deeds.

"It was a sad day for me when Everett came to me to tell me he was moving on to earn his law degree," says Carmen. "I was proud of him, but I also envied him. I'd thought after theological seminary that I might take the same path but never had."

Everett enrolled in the University of Wisconsin Law School and also began to build his own pastorate at Christ the Solid Rock Baptist Church in Madison.

"Everett possesses the charisma to inject people with a better sense of themselves. His sermons engage and encourage people, and he is a role model in his personal life. He became popular fast in Madison, because while Madisonians are often skeptical of religiosity, they also have a deep respect for people who show commitment to spiritual meaning and pursuit," says Carmen.

Eventually Everett became the Honorable Everett Mitchell, a Dane County Circuit Court Judge.

"Of course, I've told Everett that the judgeship is only a first step," laughs Carmen.

After May's death, Everett asked Carmen to speak at his church as well as teach Sunday school on Wednesday nights, an adult education class.

"When I did agree to preach, I found the experience felt like a homecoming to me," Carmen recalls. "The first time I preached in Reverend Highsmith's church back in Weirton, though, when a parishioner said, 'Amen, Brother,' I thought he wanted me to stop. Soon I realized he meant to tell me I had caught on to something and should keep going in the same direction. Since my early days of learning to speak at the pulpit in a mixed-race community, from my hometown pastor Archie Shawn and Reverend Highsmith at the AME church, which was African American, I've always found that I identify more strongly with a style of preaching that is more commonly used with African-American congregations.

"The first time I spoke at Everett's church, I went on for 45 minutes or so and then stopped on a high note. 'For a white man, you sure can preach,' Everett said to me afterwards. I took that as a great compliment. I've been back to the church many times and have found the church atmosphere so joyful."

Eventually, Carmen took up teaching the Sunday school class on Wednesday nights when he wasn't otherwise committed. He stepped in for 11 weeks in all.

"It was a great experience to be among the adult members of his church, 40 or 50 people each week, for an hour and a half or two hours at a time," Carmen says. "The experience reaffirmed my background in theology, all I'd learned and loved. I often worry that I'm losing that part of myself." Everett Mitchell helped Carmen reconnect to his spiritual roots.

In 2015, Everett Mitchell got involved with the United Way and started volunteering there in a community outreach capacity. When the United Way brought Everett on, however, he had a few conditions—he was willing to chair a community engagement committee as long as he could make a certain number of appointments.

Remembers Carmen, "So then I got a call from Everett, saying, 'Brother Carmen, I'm going to be volunteering at the United Way, and here's what we're looking to do.' Then he talked to me about community engagement and his hopes, and I said, 'That's great, but why are you calling me?'"

When Everett asked Carmen to be on the committee, he told Everett not to waste political capital aligning himself with Carmen, since he'd earned a reputation for speaking his mind, but Everett was insistent. He would not take no for an answer.

"Well," said Carmen to Everett, "then I have conditions, too."

Carmen told Everett that he'd like to see an advisory committee made up of low-income citizens who receive services from United Way agencies—a focus group of sorts—to serve as a voice and a screening process for the United Way programs.

Carmen had another condition: he wanted at least four low-income citizens to serve on the United Way board itself.

Everett loved both ideas. If Carmen would serve on the committee, Everett would try his best to get the United Way to adopt Carmen's recommendations.

Everett and Carmen were able to get low-income individuals on the advisory committee and two low-income people appointed to the board. These new members are encouraging the United Way to become the change agent they envision to secure greater justice in society.

"Everett and I have had the true luxury of becoming partners in working to change systemic injustice. He's my brother in the truest sense of the word. I just hope I live long enough to campaign for him in his next political office, which I think will be governor of Wisconsin, and to watch him be sworn in. I know that day will come," declares Carmen.

Carmen and May had built a family and support community in Madison. It was hard for Carmen to continue to be in those places without her, but the community they had built together sustained Carmen through his grief and helped prepare him for a new start.

"My faith got me through it," he concludes.

CHAPTER FIFTEEN

A New Beginning

IN MANY WAYS, CARMEN'S LIFE IS A STORY OF NEW BEGIN-
nings. As he moved from the barroom to the pulpit, he was born again,
and when he transitioned from mission work in Milwaukee to his life
with May in Madison, he reinvented himself. After losing May, he
initially felt as though he couldn't start over again, but slowly he began
to find a new hope—to imagine a new future for himself.

Carmen had probably crossed paths with Kathy Martinson countless times over the years. She had been working at the United Way in
Madison for over 30 years. In the days after May's passing, Carmen
continued his work, which was one of the ways he dealt with stress.
One day he was attending a United Way committee meeting that Judge
Mitchell had convinced him to serve on. Kathy co-chaired the committee. Carmen didn't yet know her, but she knew him.

"Somehow I'd gotten a pretty solid reputation for criticizing the
United Way," says Carmen. "I'd been known to share the viewpoint
that the organization isn't as focused as it could be on the people their
agencies serve, and not focused on the most important things that are
necessary for reducing poverty and oppression." Feeling blue that day,

having lost May just months earlier, Carmen had almost stayed home rather than attend the meeting. He recalls:

"I was sitting at home that morning having what I call shoulder fights, where one side is telling me I need to go and the other is telling me other people can handle it, I don't have to go. But I went, partly because we were hosting the meeting at Northport."

Fighting his depression, he got into his car and headed to the meeting. When Everett Mitchell got a look at him, he reassured Carmen that he could go home, that they could handle everything in his absence. Carmen agreed; he would just say hello and get back into his car. Then the conversation turned, as it often did, towards May.

Kathy Martinson overhead the two men talking about May's death, and she was moved to approach Carmen—and gave him a comforting hug.

"I lost my husband," she told Carmen. He assumed, at first, that her husband's death was as recent as May's had been. Although her husband had passed two years earlier, Kathy's empathy was very sincere. She knew what Carmen was going through.

"She offered to talk anytime," says Carmen about that meeting. "She said she would be there for me." Carmen was still receiving condolences from friends and family far and wide. He was not ready to engage with anyone outside of his immediate family just yet.

Carmen left the meeting before it started and got back in his car to go home. However, his mind stayed at the meeting. Kathy had made a strong impression. Something had stirred in him when they first met—that wonderful hug she had given him—and he couldn't shake the feeling that there was something powerful between them.

"I had a strong feeling that Kathy was going to be a big part of my life in some way," he says.

Immediately he felt guilty, to be thinking about a relationship, no matter how casual, with a woman. He shrugged off his feelings for Kathy. He was still grieving.

Several days later, he received an email from Kathy checking in on him. He responded that he was fine. Six weeks later, she emailed again, writing that she'd been thinking of him and hoped he was doing ok. He again wrote back to say he was fine. A third email arrived a few days after that. Kathy explained that she didn't know why, but she felt she needed to continue to offer her support. Before signing off, she asked Carmen if he'd like to have coffee sometime.

"At this point I thought, 'I'm never going to get rid of this lady.'" says Carmen, chuckling. Carmen, in fact, was nervous.

He figured the coffee get-together would last half an hour or so. On the way to meet her at a local coffee shop, Carmen's fears grew. What would they talk about? Carmen had not been on a date with a woman other than May for the past 44 years. Even if this was to only be a new friendship, it was a pretty big deal for Carmen.

After they greeted each other, Carmen asked Kathy about her husband. She talked for a few minutes; then she asked him about May. Four hours later, they were still talking. When they finally parted, Carmen invited her out again "You bought the first time," he said. "I'll buy the second."

Carmen struggled to play it cool, as he puts it, by waiting a few weeks to send another email. He asked if she would like to meet for another coffee. This time, he was clear about his intentions. He was still uncomfortable with starting a relationship, but the warm empathy of her hug moved him along.

"I'm not interested in a relationship beyond friendship," he wrote to Kathy. "But I like you, and I'd like to have you as a friend."

"I'd like a friend, too," she replied.

They saw each other next at a committee meeting at the United Way. Carmen was nervous seeing her among other people because of his own desire to sit with her and pick up the conversation where they had left off on their last get-together. Every time she appeared in the room to interact or deliver papers, he lost focus on the meeting.

"It was the shoulder fight all over again," says Carmen. "One side was telling me to ask her to dinner. The other was saying, 'You're not ready to get rejected, man.'"

The meeting ended, and as people were gathering their things, Carmen approached Kathy. One side of his shoulder fight declared victory: he asked her to have dinner with him the following Saturday night. Their relationship was progressing slowly, carefully.

"Yes," said Kathy. "I'd like that."

The moment she said yes, Carmen realized that he'd been expecting her to say "no thank you." He was shocked.

"You pick the spot and time, and I'll treat," said Carmen, and then he hightailed it out of the room, escaping before she had the chance to change her mind. It was like he was a teenager all over again: surprised that people would like him, or find value in a poor kid from Weirton.

Kathy emailed the next day with a restaurant suggestion. He asked if he could pick her up, but she told him she'd drive her own car and meet him at the restaurant. Carmen's mind went into overdrive. Was she meeting him at the restaurant so that she could make a quick getaway if necessary? He was unsure of himself, of whether his intentions were appropriate—it had only been about a year since May had passed.

No, said a voice inside his head. He knew a little about Kathy by this point. He knew she had worked as a quiet servant, as he puts it, to the nonprofit community, always following through. He liked this about her. He reasoned that she would follow through with their date as well. "She's an independent woman," says Carmen, recalling that date. It was hard for him to reconcile his own anxieties with her hard-earned independence.

Dinner went very well. They talked about philosophy and life, and they got into a long, deep discussion, which was also full of laughter. Carmen said to Kathy, "You're the kind of person I could care for, and if anything happened, I'd be there for you."

Recalling this moment when he spoke so frankly and emotionally, Carmen is still at a loss: "What moved me to say this on the first date? I have no idea."

Kathy looked Carmen in the eyes and said, "I would do the same thing."

"You would?" said Carmen, surprised again to find himself moving beyond friendship.

"Yes," said Kathy.

The next time they made a date to go out, Carmen asked again to pick her up, and again she declined. Navigating a new relationship was hard for Carmen. He had been so used to the type of partner he had had in May. After more than 40 years, they had just understood each other. With Kathy, it would take time, and understanding, to get to that point.

Carmen talked to his adult children, asking them what they thought about the situation. Margaret reminded him that Kathy was very much used to handling things on her own, and John noted that she was probably just as nervous as he was.

Finally, several dates later, Carmen asked again if he could pick her up, and she said yes. This seemed like a big step to Carmen. While he was used to earning and building trust in the housing communities he built, building this type of intimate trust was not something he had done since the early 1970s. That night, during dinner at a restaurant on the water, Carmen had a thought: This is much more than friendship.

They chatted and laughed all the way back to her house, but when he pulled into the driveway, he didn't even have time to cut the engine off before she slid out of her seat, closed the door, and shot up the walk and into her house.

Carmen was left sitting in an idling car, wondering what he'd done or said to have made her run away like that. He had half a mind to knock on the door and ask for an explanation, but on one shoulder, a voice said to wait. Give her time, said the voice. Carmen went home but stayed up all night because he was still perplexed and grappling with his feelings.

The following morning his daughter Margaret saw him in the kitchen. She noticed he looked like he hadn't slept. What was wrong?

He told her the story. After he finished, Margaret said, "Dad, did it ever occur to you that she might have been ready for coffee and dinner but not ready to invite you in for a drink?"

Carmen was relieved, even happy. He'd been so convinced and worried that he'd done something wrong; it was an enormous relief to realize that he was not the only one who was struggling to imagine a new life and way of being for themselves.

They went on another date. This time, they talked about their relationship and her independence and how this was a new situation for both of them, that they would need to give each other a hand.

"Kathy is a brutally honest person," says Carmen when recalling that tipping point. "She sugarcoats nothing. She's determined, decisive, and has a passion for ethical engagement. I found her ideas illuminating, and suddenly I was thinking differently. It was a different kind of love that fulfilled me." Carmen felt even closer to Kathy after that meeting, but it was a different type of closeness, and he was becoming a different person in the process.

Carmen struggled to articulate his feelings to his children. He worried that they would always think of him as belonging with their mom. Carmen looked to Kathy's relationship with her late husband's family. She and her husband had nurtured their nieces and nephews and other children in the family, and after his death, Kathy continued to be a devoted aunt. "She has always made them a priority, and still does. I admire that quality, especially at this stage of life, when another person might be turning toward herself," muses Carmen. As their relationship developed, Kathy brought Carmen into the picture. He worried about whether Kathy's family would approve, the same way he expected misunderstanding with his own family.

When he lost May, Carmen thought there was a good likelihood that he would become a hermit; it would be easy to turn inward and away from the world. Carmen's adult children had been working to prod Carmen out of the depression he was in. His friends like George Fleming tried to keep him close, but he seemed to be getting more distant. Kathy had been able to comfort Carmen and had not let him ignore her when they first started talking. Slowly, Carmen was learning to turn back toward the world, and Kathy helped him to find the way.

Carmen fell in love without knowing it.

"That first hug did something to me," says Carmen. "I couldn't shake it. It was a message to my soul—I needed to pursue this. I love her intellect, her independence, her honesty, her willingness to tell me how to improve myself—I love all of her."

Carmen was so moved by his new love that he did something he'd never done before: he wrote her love letters. As he worked out his own conflicted feelings, he felt he needed to tell her in writing that he was committed to journeying through the remainder of his life with her. They had been "ships passing in the night," he told her in one letter, and now "life had put them in the same port."

"If that didn't scare her," says Carmen with a laugh, "I knew nothing would."

It didn't scare her, and he kept writing.

"I'll bet she has 25 love letters from me at this point. I even wrote a poem for her. I got up in the middle of the night and sat at my computer, and it gushed out of me, this poem. I'll never forget it," recounts Carmen.

Those who know Carmen best would find this most surprising. In the past, he was not one to trade letters, much less poetry, but this was a new beginning for him.

"Kathy's humble," explains Carmen. "She likes herself as she is, but she doesn't make much fuss over her beauty. I wanted to tell her how beautiful she was to me, on all levels, including her beautiful soul, which is a beauty that will last forever."

Looking back, he realizes that he could have lost the chance to start over if he would have let his fear dictate his actions. It might have been easier to talk to gang leaders, HUD secretaries, and powerful politicians than to talk to Kathy, but in those conversations he was just being the person he already knew he was. With Kathy, he was becoming something new; something he hadn't thought was possible anymore.

Like his dad, Carmine, years earlier when Carmen had brought May home for the first time, he felt compelled to do something he was unaccustomed to. "I spent hours one Sunday trying to decide whether to buy her a yellow rose for friendship or a red rose for romance. Finally, I bought the yellow rose. When I gave it to her, I could tell she was relieved that it was just a friendship rose. I was somewhat disappointed, so a week later I bought her a dozen red roses to let her know how I truly felt. She told me afterwards that she'd only received roses one other time in her life."

"In this great big world full of souls, ours had found each other later in life," he marvels.

He had broken through his grief, at age 70. He no longer hid his insecurities or frailties, and in the process of sharing these with her, they grew closer.

"She soothed me," Carmen recalls. "In the past, I'd kept every-thing inside and hoped I wouldn't be discovered. Now I could say out loud how I'd been hurt and damaged, in childhood and adulthood, and Kathy heard me clearly. She made me feel whole."

Over time, Kathy shepherded him through his grief. She has also worked to bring him into her existing families—both her late husband's and her own, and Carmen feels the acceptance and love of a large, extended family again, now that most of his own extended family have passed on. He continues to learn from her example of living with and loving through grief as they take more steps to share their future together.

"I hope we never come to a place in our relationship where we stop saying 'I love you' to each other, or stop sharing a goodnight hug and a good morning kiss," Carmen reflects.

Carmen and Kathy are now married. Having recently remodeled a house together, they hope to continue to build a life together. Kathy retired from the United Way; Carmen, however, continues to work, and he plans to spend some time reflecting back on his housing ministry. With Kathy at his side, Carmen is beginning again.

"This is my first and only poem written to Kathy. One Sunday morning, I woke up, grabbed a reporter's pad, and started writing before I fell back to sleep. When I awoke again, I couldn't believe it. I typed up what I had scribbled earlier, and it formed the basis of this poem." — Carmen

The Soul Reawakens

Love, that mysterious force that unites
Bringing people together
So that the unity of the two
Creates a new dimension of being
Yet the unity becomes illusive
We must give space for each
Or the love could become intrusive
Space and place abound in the silent gaze
The mind travels in and out of the new and the old
We wonder what is coming of us
And then we discover a new oneness
Oneness crafted in love
Oneness stirred by the grasp of the soul
For the body evolves into finiteness
But the soul travels into infiniteness
And yet we yearn to understand why
When a new reality postures us to how
As we travel, our journey extends our being into memory
And we realize the time lost questioning the why
We lay our hearts before the other
We hope that the acceptance is fulfilling
Oh that we find our authenticity in the other
That we may have peace
That we may have enduring love
That life is lifted up by our blindness to imperfection

Charles Taylor

That our hearts create the warmth of thoughts
Such thoughts fuel our being
Together we posture ourselves to each other
Yet we yearn for the closeness that changes space
When we find the authenticity of our being

CHAPTER SIXTEEN

Reflections

AS CARMEN REFLECTS BACK ON HIS LIFE, ON THE VARIOUS events that shaped him and illuminated a pathway out of poverty not just for himself but for countless others who have passed through his community learning centers—a pathway toward justice—he is encouraged to continue on. He can see a community forming beyond the fencing around Northport and Packer, a ministry spreading out into the world beyond his years of service. Seeing that community being formed is a reward, one that was earned through much hard work and sacrifice, including the loss of loved ones along the way.

In 1976, on Good Friday, Carmen's oldest brother, Pat, died of a heart attack at age 48. Though they were 22 years apart in age, Carmen had always felt close to his older brother. Pat had been an idol of Carmen's growing up, namely because of all he'd done in the Weirton community, including starting a Termite baseball league, building a ballpark, and running for alderman. No Porco had ever done those things before. To Carmen, Pat exemplified the lesson that ultimately the only person who can keep you down is you, in addition to—and in spite of—institutions. He had always taken heart from Pat's example.

Pat's death had shaken Carmen to the core, and he was convinced that Pat's fate would be his own. He was sure he wouldn't live past 48 years of age. "When I turned 48, I had a heck of a tumultuous year," Carmen says. He had just broken ground on the first community learning centers in Madison, and work was tough. At home, he seemed to be butting heads with John—Pat's namesake and Carmen's oldest child—every day as John got closer to the age of 18 and thus life on his own. May had become the director of the Montessori school and therefore had less time for their long talks and drives to hash out the challenges of the day. "I held tight to the belief that if I lived for three months after turning 48, I'd be ok," says Carmen. "Then I did, and I was."

Not only did Carmen turn 48 without a fatal incident, but that year in his life also marked the point at which his work had become sustainable. His community learning centers began to offer the types of programming that he had been dreaming about since his time with Dave Stone at the Weirton Christian Center. He could start focusing on continuing the momentum that he had worked so hard to build.

All of Carmen's Weirton family is gone now; he is the sole survivor. Only a few relatives—members of the Bruno, Porco, and Bettino families—remain in Weirton today. In 2015, Carmen returned for the funeral of Cheech, his last brother to pass on, at which point he reconnected with his childhood friend John Ritter—whom Carmen had known many years ago as John Dick.

"He was the only one from the old neighborhood whom I still knew," says Carmen. "We got to reflecting on old times, and he said to me, 'I've been trapped. I'm glad you got out of here, but I'm stuck. This is what I know. I enjoy it, but I know it's empty.'"

Empty in some ways, maybe, but Carmen counts himself blessed to have grown up in a barroom in Weirton, West Virginia, a diverse community in a poor part of the country. There, he learned of the dignity of those who were labeled "poor," their lives squandered by drinking to escape the forces of oppression.

The two institutions that formed the foundation of his childhood—the barroom and the Christian Center—fueled Carmen's desire for change, not only for himself but for all people oppressed by poverty. Carmen was in his 30s when his mother, Daisy, passed away. He and his remaining brothers closed up the barroom at that time. The mill bought the property with the intention of expanding, but then it began to fail and was sold to a Japanese firm. There is now only rubble where his parent's barroom once stood, but sifting through it, one can find pieces of a life there: a brick, a shoe, and Carmen's roots.

"Throughout my childhood," says Carmen, "there was nothing but service. The barroom and restaurant served not only food but also community. Customers weren't just customers, they were family. Italians tend to share all they have: space, resources, emotions—all of it." When Carmen was still a young boy, the Porcos' bar on Avenue B became a headquarters for organizing assistance for families whose men found themselves abruptly out of work during a downturn at the mill. Carmen's mother and bar staff Jeannie and Queenie stepped up to lead the cause. They mobilized donations and used the barroom's own profits to help families buy groceries and pay bills.

This cadre of women, who went out and helped the families, were missionaries in the true sense of the word, and the money followed," recalls Carmen.

A couple of years later, when he was 11, there was another round of layoffs at the mill, and again his mother and Jeannie and Queenie stepped up to mobilize assistance. This time, though, he was a little older, and he had a better understanding of his own family's limited resources and those of others in the community.

"I asked my mother point-blank why we had to be the ones to help these people, and she said, 'Because they help you.' How did they help me? I didn't understand," recalls Carmen. "But my mother explained that they were our customers, except that customers were never just customers—we provided a service, and we looked at people in more than one way."

These were not only Carmen's roots but also the experiences that helped form his notion of a "client" that is at the center of his housing model.

Like the Porcos' customers, their employees were more than just employees. Jeannie was, as Carmen puts it, less a waitress and more a minister for the barroom community. When Daisy got sick, Jeannie and Queenie worked to cover her shifts and took care of everything. His father tried to pay them extra, but they refused.

Acts of community connection and service were all around him.

"The barroom was like a community center," Carmen recalls. "People came there to get to know one another, to feel each other's pain. It was therapeutic. And, remember, this was the so-called crudest section of town, full of poor people, people who were supposed to be mean and greedy—but they were just the opposite. They never failed to share what little they had with others." The core values that were at the center of the community Babe grew up in were the same values that he instilled in his own community centers in Madison and Milwaukee years later: he was "serving people so that they could serve themselves," he notes.

Carmen continued to learn to serve others from Dave Stone at the Weirton Christian Center. "I came to understand that doing for others is a medicine that works slowly in one's soul. Ultimately it's good for you. From a young age, I was surrounded by examples of service. Service to me is a pathway to our dignity," he adds.

"The Christian Center and Dave Stone saved me from all the negativity in my surroundings by showing me that I wasn't the sum of my behavior. I just didn't know it at the time," Carmen concludes. That illuminating notion, that Babe was more than the bad behaviors that his teachers at school had used to define him, is something that he's tried to pass along not only to his own children but to the many children and families that have passed through the community learning centers in Madison and Milwaukee. A number of his housing residents have gone on to be interns with Carmen, leaders in their own communities. They have expanded his mission into their own lives as they also work to break down the barriers and labels that continue to deprive society of a notion of shared humanity and dignity.

For Carmen, the very idea of a community means making no lines in the sand between oneself and others. Instead, the community is a circle and everyone is inside the circle. As Carmen puts it, "If one is hurting, they are all hurting."

At Alderson-Broaddus, and years later at Andover-Newton Theological School, Carmen began to realize that not everyone, including practitioners of faith, saw the world the way his family and community back in Weirton had seen it. In effect, they had faith and only faith; they didn't act in Christian ways. In grad school, he came to feel that the way he was being taught in his psychology and mission work classes to maintain professional boundaries would only create more barriers between himself and the people he wanted to serve.

His professors encouraged him to maintain the discipline it takes to make sure those boundaries remain in place. Carmen tried to work with this idea even though it rankled him. In clinical counseling, his professors pushed the theory that boundaries protect the relationship between minister and parishioner and are the only way to be helpful and effective. However, this was not the living gospel that Carmen loved; it was not discipleship.

"We do a lot of burying of our goodness," explains Carmen. "We bury it deep and are afraid to touch it, but I wanted to trust it. I believe people are good; what's bad is the way we prevent them from putting their goodness to risk. We're afraid to unleash the power of our goodness, so we marginalize goodness, which is absurd to me."

Carmen had been deeply affected by the political and racially motivated assassinations of the Kennedys and Dr. Martin Luther King Jr. in the 1960s. For Carmen, it was as if people were trying to assassinate the very soul of the country. Carmen felt some better version of the country's future was lost with those events. "We might never recover the spiritual dimension we lost with those three great leaders," he mourns. Carmen felt the country had lost its sense of goodness.

"Ministry isn't just doing for others, but helping them do for themselves, which includes helping them discover their own goodness," he says. "I believe we're better off showing them faith in their inherent goodness than showing them the problems with their behavior. Ministry is about teaching people how to tap their own goodness, not about identifying them as drug addicts or sociopaths."

All of his life, Carmen has struggled with the conflict he sees in the world between the models of service and inclusivity—people who didn't draw lines in the sand to separate themselves from bad seeds— and those who silo themselves from others. And it wasn't only Carmen's mother who demonstrated for him how to be of service in the community—it was his father, too, who taught Carmen that helping other people isn't just an option, it's a responsibility, and it's not contingent on admiring the person or their choices.

There is a saying in Italian that pretty much sums up the lessons Carmen learned from his mother and father, from Jeannie and Queenie and Bubba Jennings and Bill Smith, and from all the other men and women who made up the community in which he was raised: *Ti voglio bene*, which means simply, *I wish good things for you.*

"I vowed at 14 years old to go into the ministry, not to preach but to seek ways of delivering greater justice, to challenge the corporate world, to challenge the popular beliefs about people living in poverty.

In the right circumstances, when people have control over their own lives, they can triumph," he declares.

Retirement might be in the air for Carmen, but it's not yet a reality. His life and work are inseparable. "I'd do what I do even if I didn't get paid to do it, working in communities where people have less income but are rich in dignity and character. I hope I always have the health to do this," he states with conviction.

As he passes the torch of daily running his unique ministry to his assistant directors, Keith Atchley and his daughter, Margaret, Carmen has had time to reflect on what legacy he might eventually leave behind:

"We can't rely on leaders to change our systems. It's going to take massive numbers of human beings saying, we've had enough."

Carmen is passionate about his quest for justice, and he believes ardently that we all must do better to include the marginalized. He believes no one percent should control the country's wealth based on the idea that the one percent is more intelligent or deserving. "We have to change the way we think about community," he declares.

He has been fortunate to have built systems that create change, and people born of those systems are carrying them on into the future.

Pioneering the community learning centers and setting up the scholarship program for residents are great points of pride for Carmen, but perhaps his proudest accomplishment has been something invisible to the eye: creating institutional change based on human dignity rather than economic value. As he recalls the people, places, and events of his life, they continue to illuminate the final chapters of his life with Kathy, as well as the way forward.

CHAPTER SEVENTEEN

Epilogue: The True Church

***

"I BELIEVE I'M A PERSON WHO IS ACCEPTING OF ALL PEOPLE regardless of skin color and appearance and that I see only the souls of God," states Carmen.

This acceptance has inspired the evolution of Carmen's religious convictions and his path away from Fundamentalism. The experience of preaching and listening to preachers throughout the years caused him to start thinking about the church as an institution—its divisiveness, yes, but also its possibility to exist in the form of the "True Church," as Carmen calls it. A church that isn't limited to a building but, rather, one that is found in the streets, the barrooms, and, in his case, low-income housing complexes. He believes that pastors should minister to people as they find them because everyone is worthy of grace.

"Eventually I concluded that we've allowed our religious traditions to be cloaked in nationalistic aspirations, which voids a lot of what true Christian discipleship is about," Carmen says. "But because we institutionalize the gospel of success and materialism, we've lost the true essence of the religion that can bind instead of divide."

The key, Carmen believes, is to get back to the basic concept of the Holy Spirit. Any time he's witnessed religious people enumerate their differences from other religious people, he's moved in the direction of what he calls a radicalism based on the role of the Holy Spirit, which is the element that frees us by helping us interpret the past.

"I'm constantly searching for a better understanding of the Holy Spirit. There's legitimate division between people based on politics, abortion rights, race and equality, corporate versus individual rights, and the United States versus the world," he says. "But the Holy Spirit is about admitting we don't have a handle on the truth at all times. We're on the conveyor belt of history, and we're going to see some awful things, but we can't forget that the Holy Spirit is an agent of love that helps us integrate the journey of our existence and the creation of our community."

Carmen has witnessed so much change in his lifetime from the front lines of both the civil rights movement of the 1960s and the countercultural revolution, which in his estimation emerged in the 1970s and 80s to challenge the core beliefs of our society, to start us on a path toward understanding the true dignity of people in poverty.

"Even given the Trump administration," says Carmen, "I believe we're going to move forward, not backward. What we're living through now is the last gasp of human delusion."

He might be getting ready to step away from property management, but Carmen has great ambitions for the next phase of his life. Within the next few years, he hopes to begin work on his first book: one that will challenge the concepts of leadership of corporations and nonprofits alike.

"I hope to demonstrate to businesses that they need to learn what nonprofits are about and do, and demonstrate to nonprofits that they need to see themselves as businesses and take on different approaches. For nonprofits to continue thinking they are simply serving individual needs is a mistake; they have the responsibility of shaping community, culture, and the general society. I'd like to challenge both groups to think differently so they use their collective voices to help transform our society for the better," Carmen explains.

No matter what the next years hold for him, there's no question that his central message will outlast him.

"All organizations have a social responsibility to achieve—not simply promote—justice," he says. "Housing developments should be generators of success, not shelters of depression." Perhaps the people that he thinks needs to hear his message the most aren't sitting in corporate board rooms but in pews. He has strongly advocated for his management model as a tool for institutional change within the church.

Although Carmen's spiritual roots were sown in Catholicism and powerfully influenced by Fundamentalism during his early ministry years, he has observed for decades a more universal spirituality.

"I believe there is one Creator, one people, one shared global life, and we're all interdependent. I no longer feel a need to adhere to one ideological bent, though I still have a strong desire to search for the essence of our creation and the human community," says Carmen.

It was some of Christianity's most intrinsic assumptions that led Carmen to look for a different spiritual path. He began to hear himself using phrases like, "Accept Jesus Christ as your Lord and Savior and you will be granted eternal life."

A born questioner, Carmen stopped to really consider this basic supposition. If only those who accept Jesus Christ are eligible for salvation, then does this mean we worship a God who created everything and everyone, yet grants eternal life to some and denies it to so many? This didn't square with Carmen's deep-seated sense of justice and equality.

Carmen has come to believe, instead, in a God who embraces all of humanity unconditionally. He has come to believe, too, that the Christian schema, to which he once subscribed, has become entwined with judgment, materialism, and a certain political ideology, none of which belong in the quest for the divine, which isn't parceled out according to socioeconomic status.

"We have to be careful not to create constructs—especially religious ones—that marginalize people," he notes. "We have to see each person as an equal child of the divine Creator."

There's no one religion that has all the answers, he believes. In fact, he says, "all religious groups are probably wrong to a large degree, and the truth might be simpler than theological precepts that form the basis of our sects and groupings."

Which isn't to say that he's stopped asking what he believes is the fundamental question: Is there divinity in humanity? And if so, how do we not lose sight of it?

Carmen hasn't led a congregation of his own since his days as an associate pastor in Holden, Massachusetts. He has, however, continued to keep the title of Reverend. This was a deliberate choice on his part. The title is not only a reflection of the spiritual component of his work with people living in poverty but also a signal to the larger community that not every pastor resides in an institutional church—there are pastors living their ministries in the field of humanity, which is, in his view, the "True Church."

"The institutional church falls short of understanding that the spirit of Christ isn't tied to a structure," says Carmen. "Most of Christ's parables and travels happened outside of the church, in the Roman Empire. In the modern Christian Church, we might have missed the key lesson: that the True Church is in the core of the street and homes, where people live daily, and not where they come once a week to assert their moral superiority over others."

It is to this True Church, the homes and streets of his communities, where Carmen ministers. The parishioners of his True Church are the men and women whose lives he has personally touched. One example is a young man for whom Carmen arranged a visit to the Wisconsin Institute for Discovery at the University of Wisconsin-Madison. This young man is now intent on becoming a doctor. Carmen is able to name dozens of kids who have stayed in school and matriculated to higher education because of his guidance and confidence in them. Carmen's approach is similar to that of a counselor. He listens to people closely and gives them respect.

"One fundamental truth about people who have been oppressed by systems of poverty is that they adopt the belief that they're lacking and that's why they're marginalized. I try to show people that they're not lacking, that they have dignity and honor," he explains.

In Carmen's experience, shedding the notion that one's circumstances result from an intrinsic deficit, that people are poor because they are lazy, unskilled, or uneducated—the dominant opinion in our society—is nothing less than transformative. When people believe in their own essential value, they have much greater success.

"If we give people a nurturing environment, a stern belief that they're worthy and competent and contributors, then not only do they succeed as individuals, but they share with others," he states.

Carmen's job, as a reverend in the community, is to help people reject their own victimization and create their own destinies. And he takes this mission seriously. For Carmen, the professional is truly personal.

Carmen believes that the institutional church, or the traditional sects of Christianity and the congregations that represent them today in the United States, are among the great threats to the possibility of ever making Dr. Martin Luther King Jr.'s Beloved Community a reality.

"If we, the churchgoing people of this country, were to take not only a prophetic stance, but a stance of practical justice, we could transform systems," he maintains. "But instead our churches are wrapped up in materialism and political ideologies."

He goes a step further:

"I condemn the church strongly for what I see as a lack of effective and moral leadership. Many churches have the right intentions, but they don't risk enough in the street, where people are hurting. It's what I call cheap grace."

In Carmen's experience, cheap grace is leading the country's religious communities down a path of sustaining, rather than changing, the systems that keep people oppressed.

"Churches aren't meant to be social institutions to promote political leanings but, rather, communities to promote the divinity of all people. When they don't do this, they should be held accountable," he says.

If the traditional church has, as Carmen argues, lost its moral authority because of its tendency toward cheap grace over risk and institutional change, is there any way it might regain it?

Carmen acknowledges that the way back might be one full of obstacles. The first obstacle, he believes, is the mindset of the new generation, which is less invested in belonging to systems and more interested in individual causes and issues—which is, in Carmen's view, ultimately, another form of shortsightedness. "A person might engage with a singular issue or cause for a period of time and then go onto something else. This approach doesn't do the work of reforming the essential institutions and systems, which requires a broader, more holistic and community-focused mindset," he maintains.

The church, too, stands in the way of its own evolution when it continues to focus on political and material success, or "pseudo-success," as Carmen puts it. And this isn't purely a problem that exists on one side of the political aisle.

"Both the Left and Right are disastrous for the church because each side is only looking for an audience and not reflecting on the issues," he argues.

In an effort to provide an alternative vision, Carmen and his board of directors created what they call an Urban Center in Milwaukee to bring clergy and laity together to dialogue about the challenges facing the communities they serve: social injustice, educational obstacles, and systemic racial issues.

When the two voices come together, ideally they can develop a holistic approach to solving some of the issues that plague communities that have otherwise been abandoned by mainstream institutions—places where private educational enterprises have replaced public schools, where jobs have moved out to the suburbs, and where people are fleeing the very institutions that need the most reform.

The Urban Center embodies the foundations of Carmen's model for community development: giving the oppressed themselves a voice in developing solutions. "If every church in every community were able to form some of the same kinds of alliances, they could begin to confront the poverty in their communities," he maintains.

When he accepts a formal invitation to preach at a pulpit, it's an experience that consumes much of Carmen's consciousness for weeks or even months before the date of the engagement. His first question to himself is, "How do I speak to a person's soul?"

Carmen never ties his sermons to a given sect or institution. Instead, he always tries to inspire a person's greater sense of collective humanity, keeping in mind what Dr. Martin Luther King Jr. called the Beloved Community, a society based on justice, equality, and love of one's fellow human beings. It's this Beloved Community that Carmen appeals to in his sermons. Instead of focusing on the religious icons and biblical stories that a preacher might typically focus on, he challenges himself to speak to the greater driving force of the Creator and the divine.

Perhaps Carmen's most fully developed and widely known sermon is his exploration of the essence of Christ, which he says consists of five components: unconditional love, nonjudgmental witness, disciplined compassion, the extension of grace, and the covenant of community. If all human beings practiced these five essences, Carmen believes we could reach a higher level of consciousness.

Of course, that's not a simple goal to achieve, and it sometimes feels society is moving further from Dr. King's version of the Beloved Community than closer to realizing it. Carmen is optimistic about achieving this goal, although skeptical at the same time. It will take, he believes, a radical change of mindset with regard to our political and socioeconomic ideologies.

"We must find a way to replace the hatred, divisiveness, shortsightedness, and sense of superiority of our world with a balance toward systems and institutions that value humanity and integrity," he declares.

Carmen believes that with regard to this kind of sea change in ideology, we're playing a long-term game.

"History is owned not by humans or politicians, who often influence and report it, but by the divine Creator, who has a much broader vision for humanity, well beyond the scope of shortsightedness and inequality. We can see the Creator's power in the way nature and the environment are getting back at us now for having harmed them over time. These are parts of creation that embody a force that can supply humanity's needs, or destroy humanity if its own needs are neglected," says Carmen.

There's not a lot of modern philosophy or theology that captures Carmen's imagination or inspires his thinking. Over time, he finds himself returning more to the classics and the foundations of his own philosophical development: Walter Rauschenbusch's views on the social gospel, John Luther Adams's work on voluntary associations, and Max Stackhouse's ideas about the urban ethos. He also is an admirer of Paulo Freire's philosophy of liberation theology, an attempt to integrate the language of God and the Word and the reality of oppression, injustice, and death.

Another figure who influenced Carmen's viewpoints on the role of religion in everyday life was the Salvadoran Archbishop Oscar Romero, who spoke out against poverty, social injustice, and torture and was later assassinated. And, of course, Dr. Martin Luther King Jr.

"Dr. King was one of my greatest heroes, because of his movement in the 1960s and his attempt to raise America's consciousness. He worked with sound theology and integrity. For me, he stood out among theologians because he put the word of God into practical terms and tried to shape our society and raise our consciousness about systemic injustice," says Carmen.

"People are starting to admit that we need to learn how to see the positives of people of poverty, and to recognize that while they lack income, they do not lack character," he adds. "They may lack resources, but they clearly understand how to identify a problem and create effective solutions. This is part of my hope that people will see what I've tried to do, to the best of my ability. I have tried to fight the good fight."

People are not only listening, they are grateful for Carmen's lifetime of service and dedication to champion the plight of the poor and to seek social justice. His own life is testimony to the notion that hope can triumph over despair. He never forgot his roots, and that gave him an empathy that has guided his ministry. Carmen, a poor kid from Weirton, West Virginia, who grew up on the wrong side of town in a barroom, has led a successful ministry in transforming the lives of low-income residents and, by doing so, provided a clear example of what the True Church is all about.

APPENDIX A

Awards and Acknowledgements

Carmen has been awarded dozens of honors and accolades for his decades of working in low-income housing communities, starting as far back as 1979, when he was named Outstanding Businessman of the Year by the University of Wisconsin in Madison.

Hammer Awards

In 1997 he received not one but *four* HUD Hammer Awards, an honor created by then-Vice President Al Gore, for outstanding work in bringing technology and the Internet to segments of society that didn't otherwise have adequate access, with a focus on using technology to help people take advantage of educational and employment opportunities. Carmen was chosen specifically for the success he had experienced launching and implementing four innovative learning centers, two in Milwaukee and two in Madison.

The Hammer Award ceremony took place at the annual meeting of the Wisconsin Affordable Housing Coalition at Marquette University in Milwaukee, and the awards were presented by Dale Reynolds, the regional HUD director. Carmen was first asked to the stage to accept a Hammer Award on behalf of his work at the Northport community in Madison. He said a few words of acceptance, admired the plaque, which was signed by the vice president, and took his seat. Not a minute passed before Reynolds asked Carmen to approach the stage again—this time to receive an award on behalf of his work in the Packer community in Madison.

Carmen said a few more words, and then sat down again. He was invited to the stage a third time, this time to accept an award on behalf of his work with the Greentree community in Milwaukee. Again, he spoke and sat down. One last time, he was called to the stage to accept an award on behalf of his work in the Teutonia community in Milwaukee. Finally, after a fourth round of remarks and applause, he took his seat for the rest of the ceremony.

Mendota Elementary Award

That same year, Carmen was surprised to receive a call from the principal of Mendota Elementary, a school in Madison local to the Northport and Packer communities. He was even more surprised to learn that he was being honored by the Madison school district for his advocacy of equal treatment of low-income students and honest dialogue about race relations in the public schools—something that had gotten him into hot water with the school district in the past.

This time, he wouldn't be handed a plaque in recognition of his work; they were going to plant a tree in his honor. The tree would be a long-lasting and public display of the school district's regard for Carmen's message.

"We'd had an abrasive history, me and the schools," chuckles Carmen, "so I was surprised they wanted to honor me."

Surprised or not, Carmen showed up on the day of the ceremony, and in the presence of administrators, teachers, and members of the community, he and the school principal shoveled his tree into the ground. Many people in attendance congratulated Carmen and told him he deserved the honor. He gave a short speech about his commitment to a future of partnership with the schools in helping low-income kids succeed.

Weeks after the ceremony, Carmen found himself driving by Mendota Elementary, hoping for a glimpse of his tree. There it was, a living thing, standing tall in the schoolyard, with his name attached.

"It's incredibly meaningful to me," he says. "If this public symbol inspires someone else to stand up for issues that are important to our shared community, then it's done its job."

Champion for Change Award

In 2005, Carmen received another congratulatory phone call. This one was from HUD, the organization that had been most heavily influenced by—and stubbornly resistant to—Carmen's housing model and message. This time, he was to receive the Champion for Change Award from the national HUD office, in recognition of his role in developing, and advocating for, the Neighborhood Networks program. This award was a long time coming, since Carmen had laid the groundwork over a decade earlier.

HUD flew Carmen and his wife May to Orlando, Florida, for the ceremony, which took place at a luncheon during the annual Neighborhood Networks conference.

Starting in the late 1980s, it had taken five years for Carmen to convince HUD to allow Section 8 funds to be used to build his learning centers. The field person at the time, Robert Moser, had liked the idea, but the regulations weren't clear: there was nothing that said Carmen could use the funds the way he wanted to, and there was nothing that said he couldn't. Carmen told Moser he was going to appeal to the national office. He didn't want to go around the local office because he wanted their support.

Over the course of four years, Carmen made 37 official requests to the HUD national office. Every time, he was turned down. He was still escrowing the money he'd saved when he'd received the exemption from paying property taxes, but he couldn't use it.

Finally, after a meeting with Sen. Bill Proxmire, he had his green light. Had he given up after 20 requests and 20 rejections, or even 30, the Neighborhood Network program would almost certainly not exist today.

"My meeting with Senator Proxmire might have been the proof HUD needed to finally realize that I was not going to stop coming at them with my request," smiles Carmen. "They must have figured they might as well give in."

In presenting the award, the ceremony speaker told the audience Carmen had been "relentless," which was true, and that without Carmen's perseverance, there might never have been this magnificent change of policy within the department. The Neighborhood Networks program itself might never have come into existence.

The morning after getting the go-ahead to use the Section 8 funds for human services, Carmen called architects and scheduled meetings with residents to gather their input. Carmen's theory was that if residents had ownership over the design of the Learning Center, they'd be more likely to embrace it and help it succeed. This was in line with his philosophy that jobs created by the developments should go to residents themselves and that residents should be the ones to define the community's challenges and come up with solutions.

Five months later, they broke ground at the Northport development, and a month after that, they broke ground at the Packer development. Sue Bauman, the Madison mayor at that time, was skeptical of Carmen's approach. She called him to ask him to explain why the new centers wouldn't include gymnasiums.

"We're not handing out basketballs here," he told her. And he went on. There were several reasons why his learning centers wouldn't include gyms: First of all, the centers were designed by the residents themselves, and the residents didn't ask for a gym. Second, there were four or five gyms in the area at local schools, plus a pool, and if the mayor was willing, she could work toward getting those resources open at night, to make them available to the community.

Finally, he explained, the learning centers were meant to condition the mind, not the body. They were giving out computers and books, not basketballs. The mayor was not pleased. "And I couldn't have cared less," recalls Carmen.

Herbert Heubschmann Urban Ministry Award

Later in 2005, Carmen was given yet another award, this one from the Greater Milwaukee Interfaith Conference—the Reverend Herbert Heubschmann Urban Ministry Award—for Carmen's work with low-income families.

Before that point, Carmen hadn't been aware of Rev. Heubschmann's dedication to social justice and ending poverty in Milwaukee, but once he studied the man's accomplishments, he was doubly honored. Carmen had been working in the housing communities through Milwaukee, trying to get more of them to follow his example and build learning centers on-site and to offer more human resources; the fact that some of the faith community leaders were taking notice was a huge compliment.

Faith leaders, Carmen recalls, had been initially wary of Carmen's learning centers since they weren't focused on preaching the gospel. But Carmen persevered in demonstrating that "the gospel is better preached by action than words," as he puts it.

When he spoke at the ceremony, Carmen invoked his newfound knowledge of Rev. Heubschmann's teachings and compared the man's philosophy to Dr. Martin Luther King's Beloved Community, telling the audience that he hoped to create a more unified Milwaukee in the future.

North Star Award

In 2006, Carmen was awarded the North Star Award from the Northside Planning Council in Madison, for his work in transforming the very community the coalition serves. The award was typically not granted to individuals but to businesses and groups. The honor was bestowed on him because of his leadership in the Northport and Packer developments, where property rights and management had undergone a complete transformation under his leadership, but it was the community as a whole, he believes, who deserved the honor.

"I think I was able to demonstrate that when people in poverty are given the tools to address their own problems, they can succeed, but I felt that the award should have gone to Housing Ministries of Wisconsin, which encompasses so many people working toward the same goals, not to me personally," says Carmen.

DPI Educator of the Year

In 2007, Carmen was honored not for his social justice work in general, but specifically for his work in the area of education. He was named Educator of the Year by the Wisconsin Department of Public Instruction, for his work in education in Madison and Milwaukee.

At that time, both the Northport and Packer developments housed alternative schools, designed to assist kids who needed a higher degree of individual attention, typically for kids who had gotten in trouble in the traditional school system. These alternative schools were less rigid in structure than the traditional school system, to respond more flexibly to the individual student's needs.

"Unfortunately," says Carmen, "while the teacher-student ratio was low, which should have been a great sign, there persisted a sense among the faculty and staff that our housing community was unsafe. The staff continued to engage the kids through the negative instead of the positive."

The schools operated for three years, then closed primarily because of concerns among staff about safety. They moved the schools from the housing communities to the school district's buildings. Notably, only a small handful of students in those schools actually lived in the Packer and Northport communities.

"They couldn't say that it failed in our community because our kids are bad—that wasn't the case," recalls Carmen. "The school staff held on to their fear, in my opinion, because they didn't feel comfortable being located in a low-income community."

Carmen Porco Fund for Justice

At the 60th anniversary ceremony for the Wisconsin Council of Churches, it was announced that a fund had been created to recognize Carmen's career: the Carmen Porco Fund for Justice.

"It was a great surprise to me," notes Carmen. "I'd been involved in working to move the church toward being more prophetic and working against systemic injustice, and over the years I'd managed to encourage a number of forums to investigate systems of poverty in the institutional church. But I didn't realize that the church itself had noticed my efforts to this extent. I was floored."

Ultimately, the goal of the fund is to be an instrument to help get other programs off the ground, the kinds of programs Carmen himself might be proud to be involved in.

"I'd like to see that fund used to promote forums that highlight the positive nature of people of poverty and the potential of the church as a moral agent for the oppressed," he concludes.

Doctor of Divinity Degree: Dr. Porco

In 2008 the Central Baptist Theological Seminary awarded him a Doctor of Divinity degree, a lifetime award. The recognition coincided with an invitation for him to give the commencement speech. The honorarium was notable on its face, but even more so because typically lifetime achievement is awarded the Doctor of Ministry, which is a non-academic degree. In Carmen's case, the forums he'd led and the theological tenets he'd espoused met a standard of academic excellence worthy of the more significant honor.

"I was delighted. I believe that working in the streets involves a clear theological premise that recognizes our dignity as humans beyond the indignity of our institutions, and this honor validated my belief," he says. He still believes that his old friend, Roy Nabors, was instrumental in him being awarded this degree.

Rev. Dr. Martin Luther King, Jr. Humanitarian Award

Perhaps the most noteworthy among the legion of distinctions Carmen has received came in 2017, when he was awarded, along with his long-time friend and colleague Judge Everett Mitchell, the City-County Humanitarian Award from the Reverend Dr. Martin Luther King, Jr. Coalition. The award recognizes individuals who reflect Rev. King's values through their work in the community.

King's messages had spoken to Carmen his entire life, dating all the way back to his days in Weirton, where he and his family and friends lived under the oppression of the steel mill's dominance.

"I tried to pattern my ministry on Dr. King's theological and philosophical principles," says Carmen. "I worked all those years hoping that one day the community would recognize the ministry I've done in housing as it exemplified Dr. King's teachings about the Beloved Community, which he gave his life for. I thought that might be a way of embracing him as my hero, through my work and actions."

So the award was the ultimate validation, in a sense. And it meant even more to Carmen to receive it alongside Judge Mitchell, who had years earlier been an intern in one of Carmen's community learning centers. In a sense, Carmen was twice honored, since he had also influenced the great work of his co-recipient.

The legitimate community, as Carmen puts it, is always on the search for principled actions and people, but they don't know how to redesign their own systems—so they publicly recognize principled actions. Maybe one day the powers that recognize leadership and radical change will become the purveyors of leadership and radical change. "To me, that's the ultimate goal," Carmen says.

Carmen Porco Chair in Sustainable Business

In September 2018, Progress Through Business, an NGO, created the Carmen Porco Chair in Sustainable Business, at the University of Oxford in England. In granting this honor to Carmen, the organization stated, "Carmen has successfully brought six low-income housing communities out of default to become models of effectiveness: strong, stable, and vibrant communities that add significant value to the larger communities surrounding them.

"At the heart of these neighborhoods in both Madison and Milwaukee are five Community Learning Centers that Carmen envisioned, planned, developed, and currently directs. These centers provide an institutional basis for individuals within these communities to access the resources they need to empower them to build their own futures. Because of these accomplishments, the chair has been named in his honor and has been funded by anonymous donors." Professor John Hoffmire of Oxford University was awarded the first chair of this prestigious award in 2018, and the Reverend Carmen Porco was awarded the chair in 2019.

Convincing HUD to Pilot Carmen's Housing Ministry Model

Many of Carmen's supporters feel that his housing model should be replicated nationally and have formed a committee to petition HUD to pilot the model in five cities across the country. Carmen believes there are at least six significant challenges that must be addressed to convince HUD to support a pilot of his model:

1.   *Historically HUD's main concern was that their mortgage be paid off on time and less emphasis be placed on the human element.* Carmen believes that such a narrow view of property management doesn't serve the needs of the poor community very well. There is no specific HUD policy stating how money can be used once the mortgage is paid off. However, the need for the programs and services is present prior to the

mortgage's being paid off, and that's where permission to use funds for the model is needed.

"It would be significant if HUD encouraged property managers to set up accounts for programming and services at the beginning of their contracts," says Carmen.

If HUD's emphasis is on saving money, one would think that this model would be quite attractive to them. The model exists under the street rent caps that HUD applies to all low-income housing developments in a metropolitan area. This means that while Carmen's model provides extensive services and has a full-time staff on-site, its rent levels are still below or at the other HUD-assisted rental units' rent levels, despite these other units not supplying the level of service or investment that Carmen provides. And even when he has had a mortgage on them, Carmen's properties have remained under HUD's rent caps.

2. *HUD thinks key services should be brought into low-income housing units from outside sources, even when HUD is providing the funding.* This tends to prevent any kind of program longevity or sustainability and does not meet the needs of the low-income community. "Outside vendors, no matter how committed, make little investment into low-income communities. Too often they are in the poverty (profit) business, and that's quite different from partnering with the poor," says Carmen.

3. *Federal agencies still operate in silos, which often prevents an integrated approach that is so badly needed*

in HUD housing units. Carmen's model has the potential to show why and how an integrated approach is better.

4. *HUD could make sure that properties with a nonprofit status are getting the correct tax exemptions so they may have that extra money to put towards social programs.* "This only requires an educational campaign and providing easily accessible information," notes Carmen.

5. *HUD could create a Human Capital allocation account similar to what it has in place for physical restoration of the properties.* Mandating or allowing such accounts would encourage property managers to consider adopting the model discussed in this book.

6. *Training and leadership in low-income property management is needed to help property managers rethink how their policies and practices can support human motivation and become people-first focused.* This training is something that Reverend Porco could assist HUD in facilitating.

A pilot by HUD would allow each of the six challenges to be addressed and perhaps change policies that are currently working against the types of initiatives that are needed to impact poverty in substantive ways.

Carmen believes a pilot could be an objective way to show how his model enhances community development and enriches people's lives by providing a holistic framework of programs that are sustainable by the internal financing of the housing rents. It could also challenge the narrow mindset that restricts to outside entities the provision of services to low-income tenants instead of developing the full integration of services within the housing entity.